healthy Kids' ^ Cooking

Jean Paré

Jean Paré's childhood playhouse had pots,
pans and a real wood stove to cook on.
For more info about Jean, visit
www.companyscoming.com.

Front Cover

1. Breakfast Split, page 70
2. Fruity Milkshake, page 12
3. Healthy Chocolate Chippers, page 89
4. Go! Go! Pizza, page 114

Editor: Rita Feutl

First Printing July 2006

Library and Archives Canada Cataloguing in Publication
Paré, Jean, date
Kids' Healthy Cooking / Jean Paré.
(Original series)
Includes index.
ISBN 1-897069-02-2
1. Cookery for children–Juvenile literature. I. Title.
II. Title: Kids' healthy cooking. III. Series: Paré, Jean,
    date - Original series.
TX652.5.P378 2006   j641.5'123   C2006-900300-9

Published by
Company's Coming Publishing Limited
2311 – 96 Street
Edmonton, Alberta, Canada T6N 1G3
Tel: 780-450-6223 Fax: 780-450-1857
www.companyscoming.com

We gratefully acknowledge the following suppliers for their generous support of our Test Kitchen and Photography Studio:

Broil King Barbecues
Corelle®
Hamilton Beach® Canada
Lagostina®
Proctor Silex® Canada
Tupperware®

Our special thanks to the following businesses for providing props for photography:

Anchor Hocking Canada
Canadian Tire
Canhome Global
Casa Bugatti
Cherison Enterprises Inc.
Danesco Inc.
Michaels The Arts & Crafts Store
Pfaltzgraff Canada
Pier 1 Imports
Stokes
The Bay
The Dazzling Gourmet
Wal-Mart Canada Inc.
Wiltshire®
Winners Stores

Note to Parents

The word is out: our children need to eat better. But at Company's Coming, we know that most kids would sooner snack on a chocolate bar than a carrot stick. So we surveyed youngsters to find out what they were eating, and then set out to make their favourites healthier. In *Kids' Healthy Cooking*, you won't find alfalfa sprouts and carob chips. Instead, children will recognize these healthier versions of more than 80 breakfast, lunch and snack recipes that they can make themselves.

Kids' Healthy Cooking also offers youngsters a fun, personal way to look at nutrition. We've related it to their bodies, showing them, for example, how eating protein keeps their muscles strong, breakfasts make their brains work better, and fruit and vegetables add a healthy glow to their skin and hair. Each body-part chapter is full of nutritional info, trivia facts and kid-friendly jokes, as well as related recipes they'll love to make on their own.

But they'll still need some guidance from you. Before you set your youngsters loose in the kitchen, make sure you've gone over ground rules. If they have allergies or dietary restrictions, let them know what's allowed.

Establish which appliances are off limits. Are you comfortable with them using the oven and stove, or just the microwave? Which knives are OK? Can your kids handle cooking spray, or would you rather show them how to grease surfaces with oil or butter? Make sure they go over the safety information on page 7 before they start.

To make it easy on kids, we often called for ingredients such as pre-cut deli cheese slices. But if your child can cut a slice from a block of Cheddar, don't make an extra trip to the grocery store.

We also varied serving sizes. Some are one-portion recipes just for them, and you may have to nudge them to put away leftover

ingredients. Others recipes are designed to be shared—who knows, you might be invited to sit down to a home-cooked meal in your own kitchen!

Kids' Healthy Cooking is all about letting kids have fun in the kitchen, learning to make healthier dishes they'll want to eat. What a great gift to give to our children!

Jean Paré

Nutrition Information Guidelines

Each recipe is analyzed using the most current version of the Canadian Nutrient File from Health Canada, which is based on the United States Department of Agriculture (USDA) Nutrient Database.

- Milk used is 1% M.F. (milk fat), unless otherwise stated.
- Cooking oil used is canola oil, unless otherwise stated.
- Deli cheese and cold cut slices were analyzed as 1 1/2 oz. (43 g) unless otherwise stated.
- Ingredients indicating "sprinkle," "optional," or "for garnish" are not included in the nutrition information.

Margaret Ng, B.Sc. (Hon.), M.A.
Registered Dietitian

Table of Contents

Egg-O-Rama, Fruity Milkshake, Cheesy Apple Melt, Chicken Samosa Boats, Cheesy Broccoli Soup, Hammy Hammocks, Grilled Cheese Sandwich, Hotza Mozza Sticks, Mango Lassi, Banana Monkey Crunch

Pump It Up

Berry Creamy Waffles, Fridge Fruit Salad, Tikki Tikki Muffins, Rabbit's Soup, Mexi-Taters, Chop Chop Suey, Piggy Bank Popcorn, Pineapple Fizz, Plushie, Banana Berry "Ice Cream"

Fuel Your Think Tank

Broken-Hearted Egg Toast, Nut And Honey Granola, Smart Shake, Frittata Muffins, Ocean Burgers, Under-The-Sea Taco, Seafood Chowder, Sun-Dried Tomato Dip, Frozen Banana Rocket, Frosty Fruit Soup

Power Play

Big Breakfast, Hakuna Frittata, Corn Tomato Chowder, Fiesta Pizza, Budding Chef's Salad, Cheesy Lunch Lasagne, Thousand On A Raft, Egg Drop Soup, Tofu Taco Dip, Muchos Nachos

The Ins & Outs of Eating

Quick Fruit Crisp, Weekend Wake-Up Call, Breakfast Split, Hawaiian Toasts, Nutty Noodles, Beany Burrito, Mexi-Bean Dip, Almond Berry Trifle, Coconut Crisps, Cranberry Almond Chewies

Go with the Flow

The Cover Story

Go! Go! Go!

Watch for our handy clock with each recipe! It will help you find a great breakfast, lunch or snack idea.

breakfast

lunch

snack

Hi! I'm Cookie! To help you with kitchen questions, check out my tips throughout the cookbook. I'm here to tell you everything from how to make perfect scrambled eggs to why you need to poke potatoes before you microwave them.

A kid walks into the doctor's office with a pickle in one ear, a cucumber in the other and a carrot up one nostril.

"Doctor! What's wrong with me?"

"Well it's obvious," says the doctor, "You're not eating right."

I bet you've heard adults go on about how kids these days don't eat right. And you probably even know the basics: eat from the four food groups (see below), don't pig out, and chew with your mouth closed.

But if you've always wondered *why* you need to eat right (who looks good with a carrot up their nose?), this is the cookbook for you. You'll find out how the food you eat affects different parts of your body, and then you can try out some delicious recipes to see for yourself. But remember: don't just concentrate on, say, the muscle chapter of the book. Check out the other sections so you're looking after ALL of you. Balance is the key to eating right!

The **four food groups** are:

a) pretzels, salsa, nachos and peanuts

b) fruit and vegetables, grains, dairy, and meat and meat alternatives

c) brownies, sundaes, cakes and cookies

d) potato chips, popcorn, pickles and a partridge in a pear tree

Answer: b

Bossy Safety Stuff

I know, I know, you hate being told what to do, but here's why:

> Make sure the adults are OK with you cooking. And it helps to check if you can use up ingredients. (If you use up the cheese, how is Mom supposed to make her famous liver soup for supper?)

> Tie up long hair. It's gross to find a strand around the pasta, and it's worse to have it catch in a blender or singe on a burner.

> Same goes for loose clothing (well, you might not find it in the pasta). But tuck in those shirts and roll up those sleeves.

> Wash your hands with soap at the start, and every time you change ingredients. Grey cookie dough? Yuck! Onion-flavoured grey cookie dough? Double yuck!

> Dry your hands before plugging in appliances or touching sockets, otherwise you'll have an electrifying experience.

> Use oven mitts whenever you handle hot dishes or pans.

> Turn saucepan and frying pan handles toward the centre or the back of the stove so people can't knock them off the stove.

> Turn off the stove and oven when you're done.

> Be careful with hot water. Don't overfill a pan, and if it's too heavy for you to lift, please ask a grown-up for help.

> Wipe up spills, especially greasy ones, as soon as possible to prevent an indoor skating rink. Hot, soapy water will do the trick.

> If younger brothers and sisters are "helping," keep them away from sharp knives and hot stoves.

Basic Cooking Stuff

> Wash your hands before you start (see Bossy Safety Stuff, page 7).

> Read the recipe all the way through before you start.

> Gather your ingredients and equipment first. This prevents you from scrambling for an egg lifter while the burger is burning.

> Wash your fruit and vegetables before cooking or eating.

> Use the size of pot/pan/plate, etc. that it says in the recipe. We've tested the recipes this way to make sure you'll succeed.

> Use the right measuring tools. See page 9 for instructions.

> Do one recipe step at a time. The numbers beside our ingredients match the steps to keep you on track. Don't skip steps.

> As you finish with bowls and pans, pop them in the dishwasher or rinse them out. This prevents a humungous mess at the end.

> Did we mention a mess? Clean up when you're done, or you may be banned from the kitchen (except to wash everyone else's dishes)!

Ingredient Stuff

Say you're all ready to make the Cheesy Apple Melt, and you discover there are no deli Cheddar cheese slices in the fridge. If your parents let you cut your Cheddar cheese block, you're all set to go. Just remember to cut thin slices, and have enough to cover the palm of an adult's hand.

The same goes for chocolate milk. You can make your own with regular milk and chocolate powder or syrup.

Don't substitute just anything, though. Ask an adult if you're thinking about using another ingredient for one that's listed in a recipe.

Kitchen Tools and What to Do with Them

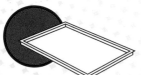

Baking Sheet
This has sides. It's sometimes called a jelly-roll pan. Just the thing when you're baking something that might roll off a cookie sheet.

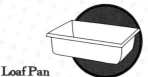

Loaf Pan
Normally for meatloaves and bread, its shape is useful for other recipes too.

Measuring Spoons
These are just tiny measuring cups. Make sure the contents are level, unless the recipe calls for a "heaping" spoon.

Saucepan
Sometimes called a pot. Make sure you use the size called for in the recipe. Turn the handle toward the centre of the stove so the pot can't be knocked off when someone walks by.

Wire Rack
Good for cooling baked items by letting air flow underneath.

Cookie Sheet
Cookies slide off easily onto a wire rack because the sheet has no sides.

Dry Measures
Use these to measure all ingredients that aren't liquid. To measure flour properly, spoon it into your cup, and then level off the extra flour with the straight side of a knife.

Muffin Pan
Our recipes call for a pan that bakes 12 muffins.

Strainer
Easily separates solids from liquids. Do it over a sink to keep spills to a minimum.

Oven with Rack Positions
It's important to follow the recipe instructions for rack positions.

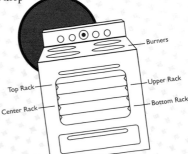

Burners

Top Rack — Upper Rack

Center Rack — Bottom Rack

Grater
Perfect for grating carrots or cheese. Go slowly as you finish grating so your knuckles don't get caught.

Liquid Measures
Fill your liquid and set your cup on an even surface. Check at eye level to see if the liquid reaches the mark. These cups have a rim so you won't spill liquids after you've measured them.

Pancake Lifter
Also called an egg lifter.

Whisk
A tool that mixes ingredients and breaks up lumps.

Build Dem Bones
Calcium for Your Skeleton

Picture yourself with no bones. Not a pretty sight, is it? Just a sack of skin stuffed with blood and organs, blobbing along the ground. Make no bones about it, you need a skeleton to shape your body and protect important organs like your brain from being bumped or bruised.

You're born with about 300 bones, but you'll have only 206 by the time you're in your 20s. That's because as you grow, some of your bones, like the ones in your skull, fuse together. While you're in your teens, your bones become bigger and harder. (If last season's jeans won't reach your ankles anymore, it's a sign your bones are getting longer!) To grow strong, your skeleton needs exercise: weight-bearing sports such as basketball, soccer, dancing and even walking the dog help make dem bones powerful.

Calcium is key to good bones. Without it, they can become brittle and break easily. Dairy products such as milk, yogurt, cheese and ice cream are great sources. You can also find it in broccoli, oatmeal and almonds.

Your teeth need calcium too. They're a part of your skeletal system but aren't counted as bones. Teeth are made of dentin and covered with a coating of enamel. Enamel is the strongest substance in your body. Now that's something to chew on!

Egg-O-Rama

Feeling bone-weary when you wake up? A topping of cheese on this egg-and-waffle breakfast will have your skeleton doing a happy dance.

Get It Together: microwave-safe plate, sharp knife, cutting board, small bowl, fork, measuring spoons, small frying pan, mixing spoon

1. Frozen waffle	1	1
Small tomato, sliced	1	1
Salt, sprinkle		
Pepper, sprinkle		
2. Large egg	1	1
Cooking oil	1/2 tsp.	2 mL
3. Process Cheddar cheese slices	2	2

1. Toast the waffle. Place it on the plate. Arrange the tomato slices on the waffle. Sprinkle with salt and pepper.

2. Break the egg into the bowl. Beat with the fork until the egg is bubbly on top. Heat the cooking oil in the frying pan on medium for 3 minutes. Pour the egg into the pan. Heat and stir for about 1 minute until the egg is cooked. Remove the pan from the heat. Spoon the scrambled egg on top of the tomato.

3. Place the cheese on top of the scrambled egg. Microwave, covered, on high (100%) for about 20 seconds until the cheese is melted. Serves 1.

1 serving: 376 Calories; 23.9 g Total Fat (8.3 g Mono, 3 g Poly, 10.6 g Sat); 264 mg Cholesterol; 22 g Carbohydrate; 3 g Fibre; 19 g Protein; 967 mg Sodium

Pictured on page 10.

So here's the deal on perfect scrambled eggs: cook them just long enough so the liquid egg becomes solid, but not so long that they're dry and crumbly. It's OK if the eggs are still a little shiny. When they're done, remove the eggs from the frying pan right away to prevent them from overcooking.

Fruity Milkshake

Who thinks milk is boring? Frozen fruit makes a delicious calcium-rich shake. Team it with toast for a well-rounded breakfast.

Get It Together: liquid measures, dry measures, blender, large glass

1.			
Milk		3/4 cup	175 mL
Frozen whole strawberries		1/2 cup	125 mL
Vanilla frozen yogurt		1/2 cup	125 mL

1. Put all 3 ingredients into the blender. Cover with the lid. Process until smooth. Pour into the glass. Serves 1.

1 serving: 284 Calories; 7.8 g Total Fat (2.2 g Mono, 0.3 g Poly, 4.9 g Sat); 18 mg Cholesterol; 44 g Carbohydrate; 2 g Fibre; 11 g Protein; 161 mg Sodium

Pictured on front cover and on page 13.

Bright Idea: Instead of strawberries, use frozen raspberries, blueberries or whatever's on hand. To make your own frosty fruit, see page 1 0 3.

What do you call a nervous cow? A milkshake.

Cheesy Apple Melt

Eating the apple peel (wash it first!) means half the work and twice the fibre. Remember that the thinner the apple slices, the softer they'll be after cooking.

Get It Together: microwave-safe plate, sharp knife, cutting board

1.		
Raisin bread slice	1	1
Thin apple slices	8	8
Deli Cheddar cheese slices	2	2

1. Toast the bread. Place it on the plate. Arrange the apple slices on the toast. Place the cheese on top. Microwave, uncovered, on high (100%) for about 30 seconds until the cheese is melted. Serves 1.

1 serving: 261 Calories; 15.2 g Total Fat (4.6 g Mono, 0.6 g Poly, 9.2 g Sat); 44 mg Cholesterol; 19 g Carbohydrate; 2 g Fibre; 13 g Protein; 362 mg Sodium

Pictured on page 13.

No microwave? No problem! Put the sandwich on an ungreased baking sheet and broil on the top rack in the oven for about 2 minutes until the cheese is melted. Or place it on a broiler pan in a toaster oven and broil for 2 minutes.

Top: Fruity Milkshake, page 12
Bottom: Cheesy Apple Melt, page 12

Chicken Samosa Boats

The scent of samosas (deep-fried pastries stuffed with meat or vegetables) wafts through busy streets in India. We've popped the filling into a potato skin for an easy version.

Get It Together: fork, oven mitts, sharp knife, cutting board, teaspoon, medium bowl, microwave-safe plate, dry measures, measuring spoons, mixing spoon, grater

1. Large unpeeled potato		1	1
2. Grated medium Cheddar cheese		1/2 cup	125 mL
Mayonnaise		2 tbsp.	30 mL
Curry powder		1/4 tsp.	1 mL
Pepper		1/8 tsp.	0.5 mL
3. Frozen peas		1/4 cup	60 mL
Diced cooked chicken		1/4 cup	60 mL
4. Grated medium Cheddar cheese		1/4 cup	60 mL

1. Poke the fork into the potato in several places. Microwave, uncovered, on high (100%) for 3 minutes. Use the oven mitts to turn the potato over. Microwave for another 3 minutes. The potato is cooked when you can easily poke it with the fork. Let the potato stand for about 5 minutes until cool enough to handle. Cut the potato in half lengthwise. Use the teaspoon to scoop out potato flesh from both halves into the bowl. Leave a little bit of the potato flesh attached to the skins so they don't tear. Place the potato skins on the plate. Set aside. Mash the potato flesh in the bowl with the fork.

2. Add the next 4 ingredients. Stir until well mixed.

3. Add the peas and chicken to the potato mixture. Stir. Spoon the chicken mixture into the potato skins.

4. Sprinkle with the second amount of cheese. Microwave, covered, on high (100%) for about 2 minutes until the cheese is melted. Serves 2.

1 serving: 425 Calories; 28 g Total Fat (11.1 g Mono, 4.6 g Poly, 11 g Sat); 75 mg Cholesterol; 22 g Carbohydrate; 3 g Fibre; 21 g Protein; 400 mg Sodium

Pictured on page 15.

Give Mom a break! Poking small holes in the potato allows steam to escape during cooking so the potato won't explode.

Cheesy Broccoli Soup

Cheese, milk and broccoli—a triple play for strong bones! Serve this creamy soup with whole-grain muffins or crackers for a complete lunch.

Get It Together: can opener, medium saucepan, whisk, mixing spoon, dry measures

1. Can of condensed Cheddar cheese soup	10 oz.	284 mL
Milk (1 soup can)	10 oz.	284 mL
2. Chopped broccoli	2 cups	500 mL

1. Put the soup into the saucepan. Slowly add the milk, stirring constantly with the whisk until the mixture is smooth.

2. Add the broccoli. Heat and stir on medium for about 5 minutes, stirring occasionally, until the soup is steaming but not bubbling. Turn down the heat to medium-low. Cook, uncovered, for about 10 minutes, stirring occasionally, until the broccoli is tender. Serves 2.

1 serving: 274 Calories; 14.5 g Total Fat (4 g Mono, 0.6 g Poly, 9 g Sat); 41 mg Cholesterol; 25 g Carbohydrate; 2 g Fibre; 14 g Protein; 1251 mg Sodium

Pictured on page 17.

To see if vegetables are finished cooking, poke through their thickest part with a fork. As soon as you can easily push the fork through, the vegetables are "fork-tender" and ready to eat.

Chicken Samosa Boats, page 14

Hammy Hammocks

A calcium boost cradled in tiny lettuce hammocks.
No time to rest? Roll up your hammocks in whole
wheat tortilla "blankets" for a quick getaway.

Get It Together: grater, sharp knife, cutting board, dry measures, measuring spoons, small bowl, mixing spoon, dinner plate

1.		
Grated medium Cheddar cheese	1/2 cup	125 mL
Chopped ham	1/3 cup	75 mL
Cream cheese, softened	1 tbsp.	15 mL
Chopped dill pickle	1 tbsp.	15 mL
Prepared mustard	1/2 tsp.	2 mL
2. Small lettuce leaves	6	6

1. Put the first 5 ingredients into the bowl. Stir until well mixed.

2. Place the lettuce leaves on the plate. Spoon the cheese mixture into the leaves. Serves 1.

1 serving: 332 Calories; 25.5 g Total Fat (8 g Mono, 1.4 g Poly, 14.5 g Sat); 90 mg Cholesterol; 5 g Carbohydrate; 1 g Fibre; 21 g Protein; 1091 mg Sodium

Pictured on page 17.

Bright Idea: Lettuce (get it?) consider new flavours. Instead of Cheddar cheese, try grated Swiss or Gouda. Cooked turkey or roast beef are just as good as ham. Use whatever's in the fridge!

Calcium is:

a) an old stadium in Italy

b) a person from Calgary, Alberta

c) an important mineral for healthy bones and teeth

d) the name of a heavy-metal rock band

Answer: c

Top: Cheesy Broccoli Soup, page 15
Centre: Hammy Hammocks, above
Bottom: Grilled Cheese Sandwich, page 19

Grilled Cheese Sandwich

The perfect sandwich for dipping into a steaming bowl of tomato soup. If you make one for your sister, she might even help with the dishes!

Get It Together: table knife, measuring spoons, small frying pan, pancake lifter

1. Whole wheat bread slices	2	2
Butter, softened	2 tsp.	10 mL
2. Deli Cheddar cheese slices	2	2

1. Spread the bread slices with butter.

2. Heat the frying pan on medium until a few drops of water sprinkled on the pan sizzle immediately. Place 1 bread slice, buttered-side down, in the pan. Place the cheese on the bread. Place the other bread slice, buttered-side up, on top of the cheese. Cook for about 1 1/2 minutes until the bottom is golden. Use the lifter to check. Press the lifter on the top bread slice so it will stick to the melting cheese. Carefully turn the sandwich over. Cook for another 1 to 1 1/2 minutes until both sides are golden. Serves 1.

1 serving: 410 Calories; 26.7 g Total Fat (7.9 g Mono, 1.3 g Poly, 15.9 g Sat); 73 mg Cholesterol; 27 g Carbohydrate; 4 g Fibre; 18 g Protein; 688 mg Sodium

Pictured on page 17.

YODELLER'S LUNCH: Grill Swiss cheese between rye bread slices.

MAMMA MIA: Grill mozzarella cheese and tomato slices between whole wheat bread slices.

SPICY MEXICANO: Grill jalapeño Monterey Jack cheese, sprinkled with chopped red pepper, between multi-grain bread slices.

Didya know: the **smallest bone** in your body is in your ear? It's commonly called the **stirrup bone,** and is **half the size** of a grain of rice!

Top left: Mango Lassi, page 21
Bottom: Hotza Mozza Sticks, page 20

Hotza Mozza Sticks

A gooey snack for sharing—but no double dipping in the pizza sauce! These need to go into the freezer before cooking so that the cheese doesn't ooze out of the crumb coating.

Get It Together: foil, baking sheet with sides, cooking spray, dry measures, measuring spoons, 3 small bowls, mixing spoon, fork, sharp knife, cutting board, oven mitts, wire rack

1. Cornflake crumbs	1/2 cup	125 mL
Chili powder	1/4 tsp.	1 mL
2. Large egg	1	1
3. All-purpose flour	1 tbsp.	15 mL
4. Package of mozzarella cheese sticks (8 per package)	6 oz.	168 g
5. Pizza sauce	1/2 cup	125 mL

1. Cover the baking sheet with foil. Grease with the cooking spray. Put the cornflake crumbs and chili powder into 1 of the small bowls. Stir until well mixed. Set aside.

2. Break the egg into the second small bowl. Beat with the fork until the egg is bubbly on top. Set aside.

3. Put the flour into the third small bowl.

4. Cut each cheese stick crosswise into 3 equal pieces so that you have a total of 24 pieces. Working with 1 piece at a time, roll the cheese in the flour until coated, and then put it on the fork. Dip the cheese into the beaten egg until coated. Let any extra egg drip off the cheese back into the bowl. Roll the cheese in the crumb mixture until coated. Place the coated cheese on the baking sheet. When all the pieces are done, put the baking sheet in the freezer for at least 1 hour.

5. Place the oven rack in the centre position. Turn the oven on to 450°F (230°C). Lightly spray the coated cheese with the cooking spray to help it brown. When the oven is hot, bake for about 3 minutes until the coating is crisp and the cheese is warm. Turn the oven off. Remove the baking sheet to the wire rack. Let stand for 5 minutes. Serve the cheese sticks with the pizza sauce. Serves 4.

(continued on next page)

1 serving: 233 Calories; 12.3 g Total Fat (4.2 g Mono, 0.9 g Poly, 6.4 g Sat); 88 mg Cholesterol; 19 g Carbohydrate; 1 g Fibre; 12 g Protein; 466 mg Sodium

Pictured on page 18.

Keep an eye on the clock or use a kitchen timer to make sure you don't overcook the mozza sticks, otherwise the cheese oozes out and makes a mess.

Mango Lassi

A lassi is a sweet yogurt drink that goes great with a spicy meal. Lasso this lassi for an after-school snack!

Get It Together: dry measures, liquid measures, blender, large glass

1. Frozen mango pieces, page 103	1 cup	250 mL
Vanilla yogurt	3/4 cup	175 mL
Milk	1/2 cup	125 mL

2. Ground cinnamon, sprinkle

1. Put the first 3 ingredients into the blender. Cover with the lid. Process until smooth. Pour into the glass.

2. Sprinkle with cinnamon. Serves 1.

1 serving: 346 Calories; 5.5 g Total Fat (1.6 g Mono, 0.3 g Poly, 3.4 g Sat); 16 mg Cholesterol; 66 g Carbohydrate; 3 g Fibre; 13 g Protein; 180 mg Sodium

Pictured on page 18.

Bright Idea: How about peaches with peach yogurt, or strawberries with strawberry yogurt for a different taste?

Remember, don't be a **bonehead** and eat just **one type of food!** Your body **needs** a healthy balance of **different foods.**

Banana Monkey Crunch

*Bone up on calcium with the yogurt in this yummy snack.
There's enough for friends, or save some for breakfast.
Top with the granola and banana just before eating.*

Get It Together: can opener, large bowl, dry measures, whisk, mixing spoon,
6 dessert bowls, sharp knife, cutting board

1. Can of crushed pineapple	14 oz.	398 mL
2. Vanilla yogurt	3 cups	750 mL
Box of instant vanilla pudding powder	1	1
(4 serving size)		
3. Granola	1 cup	250 mL
Medium bananas, sliced	2	2

1. Drain the juice from the pineapple into the large bowl. Set aside the pineapple.

2. Add the yogurt and pudding powder to the pineapple juice. Beat with the whisk for about 2 minutes until the mixture is smooth and thick. Add the crushed pineapple. Stir well. Spoon into the dessert bowls.

3. Sprinkle with the granola. Top with the banana. Serves 6.

*1 serving: 356 Calories; 8.2 g Total Fat (2.3 g Mono, 3 g Poly, 2.6 g Sat); 7 mg Cholesterol;
67 g Carbohydrate; 3 g Fibre; 8 g Protein; 322 mg Sodium*

Pictured on page 23.

Bright Idea: Plain yogurt instead of vanilla yogurt makes this recipe a little
less sugary.

What did one **skeleton say** to the **other skeleton**
at lunchtime?

Bone-appétit!

Banana Monkey Crunch, above

Pump It Up
Low-Fat Foods for Your Heart

Make a fist. That's the size of your heart. Pretty small for a muscle that keeps your whole body pumped and ready to do whatever you need it to do, whether it's running for the bus or holding this book.

Your heart sends blood circling around your body, delivering nutrients and oxygen from your lungs through your arteries, right down to your fingertips and toes. Then it pumps it back through your veins, and the whole cycle starts again.

Place your fingers on the wrist of your other hand below the thumb. Can you feel your heart pumping blood? Each beat is called a pulse. When you exercise, feel excited or your bratty brother's jumped out from the closet at you, your pulse speeds up because your body needs more oxygen. In one day, your heart can beat more than 100,000 times!

Foods with lots of fat block up your arteries and make it hard for your heart to send out oxygen and nutrients. Help it stay healthy by choosing foods lower in fat. And exercise that muscle by doing something active; your heart will thank you from the bottom of its…heart!

Berry Creamy Waffles

Berry Creamy Waffles

Waffling about high fibre? Check out high-fibre waffles—their nutty flavour pairs up well with berries and yogurt for a heart-y breakfast.

Get It Together: dry measures, small microwave-safe bowl, mixing spoon, oven mitts, dinner plate, measuring spoons, table knife

1. Frozen mixed berries	1/4 cup	60 mL
Applesauce	1/4 cup	60 mL
2. Frozen waffles	2	2
3. Vanilla yogurt	6 tbsp.	100 mL

1. Put the berries and applesauce into the bowl. Microwave, covered, on high (100%) for 1 minute. Stir. Microwave on high (100%) for about 30 seconds more until hot. Use the oven mitts to remove the bowl from the microwave. Set aside.

2. Toast the waffles. Place 1 waffle on the plate.

3. Spread 2 tbsp. (30 mL) of the yogurt on the waffle. Spread 1/2 the berry mixture on the yogurt. Put the second waffle on top of the berry mixture. Spread another 2 tbsp. (30 mL) of the yogurt on the second waffle. Top with the remaining berry mixture. Spoon the remaining yogurt onto the centre of the berry mixture. Serves 1.

1 serving: 329 Calories; 8.1 g Total Fat (2.9 g Mono, 2.2 g Poly, 2.2 g Sat); 22 mg Cholesterol; 57 g Carbohydrate; 5 g Fibre; 9 g Protein; 639 mg Sodium

Pictured on page 24.

Bright Idea: Any berries, fresh or frozen, will make this waffle stack taste great. What's in the freezer?

W hat do you get when **3 6 2 blueberries** try to leave school at the same time?

Blueberry jam!

Fridge Fruit Salad

The heart of the matter is that this refreshing salad is terrific with yogurt and toast for a balanced breakfast. Try different fruits for variety.

Get It Together: can opener, strainer, medium bowl, cutting board, sharp knife, measuring spoons, dry measures, mixing spoon

1. Can of sliced peaches	14 oz.	398 mL
2. Honey	2 tbsp.	30 mL
Ground cinnamon, just a pinch		
3. Chopped cantaloupe	2 cups	500 mL
Chopped honeydew	1 cup	250 mL
Halved seedless grapes	1 1/2 cups	375 mL

1. Drain the juice from the peaches into the bowl. Chop the peaches. Set aside.

2. Add the honey and cinnamon to the juice in the bowl. Stir.

3. Add the peaches and remaining 3 ingredients. Stir until the fruit is coated. Serves 5.

1 serving: 117 Calories; 0.4 g Total Fat (0 g Mono, 0 g Poly, 0 g Sat); 0 mg Cholesterol; 31 g Carbohydrate; 2 g Fibre; 2 g Protein; 14 mg Sodium

Pictured on page 27.

Bright Idea: Make your own fruit snack cups for school lunches! Put this salad into small airtight containers. They will keep in the refrigerator for up to 5 days so you can add one to your lunch bag each day.

Why did the skeleton not want to play basketball?
Her heart wasn't in it.

Top: Fridge Fruit Salad, above
Bottom: Tikki Tikki Muffins, page 28

Tikki Tikki Muffins

*This chunky muffin is packed with
fruit and sweet, tropical flavours.
Don't be heartless—share!*

Get It Together: muffin pan, cooking spray, large bowl, dry measures, measuring spoons, mixing spoon, sharp knife, cutting board, small bowl, fork, can opener, strainer, oven mitts, wooden toothpick, wire rack

1.		
All-purpose flour	1 1/2 cups	375 mL
Quick-cooking rolled oats	1/2 cup	125 mL
Brown sugar, packed	1/4 cup	60 mL
Baking soda	1 tsp.	5 mL
Ground cinnamon	1/2 tsp.	2 mL
Salt, sprinkle		
2.		
Chopped dried apple	1 cup	250 mL
Chopped dried apricot	1 cup	250 mL
3.		
Large egg	1	1
Can of crushed pineapple, well drained	14 oz.	398 mL
Unsweetened applesauce	1 cup	250 mL
Cooking oil	1/4 cup	60 mL

1. Place the oven rack in the centre position. Turn the oven on to 375°F (190°C). Grease the muffin cups with the cooking spray. Set aside. Put the first 6 ingredients into the large bowl. Stir well.

2. Add the apple and apricot. Stir until coated. Dig a hole in the centre of the flour mixture with the mixing spoon.

3. Break the egg into the small bowl. Beat the egg a little with the fork. Add the remaining 3 ingredients. Stir until well mixed. Pour into the hole in the flour mixture. Stir just until the flour mixture is moistened. Fill the muffin cups to the top with the batter. Bake for 20 to 25 minutes until golden and the toothpick inserted straight down into the centre of a muffin comes out clean. Remove the pan to the wire rack. Let stand for 5 minutes. Turn the oven off. Transfer the muffins from the pan to the wire rack to cool. Makes 12 muffins.

1 muffin: 208 Calories; 5.8 g Total Fat (3.1 g Mono, 1.7 g Poly, 0.6 g Sat); 18 mg Cholesterol; 37 g Carbohydrate; 3 g Fibre; 3 g Protein; 123 mg Sodium

Pictured on page 27.

(continued on next page)

It's always a good idea to check your baking for doneness at the earlier time given in a recipe, because you don't want your baking to dry out. If there's still wet batter on your toothpick, bake for another 5 minutes and test again with another pick.

Rabbit's Soup

A soup any bunny would love! Drizzle some ranch dressing in a fun pattern as garnish or add crackers for some crunch.

Get It Together: large saucepan, dry measures, liquid measures, mixing spoon, ladle, blender

1. Baby carrots	2 cups	500 mL
Prepared vegetable broth	2 cups	500 mL
2. Ice cubes	6	6
Chilled vegetable juice	1 cup	250 mL

1. Put the carrots and broth into the saucepan. Heat on medium-high until the broth is bubbling. Turn down the heat to medium. Cook, uncovered, for about 20 minutes, stirring occasionally, until the carrots are soft. Remove from the heat.

2. Add the ice cubes. Stir until melted. Add the juice. Stir. Carefully ladle into the blender. Cover with the lid. Process until smooth. Return to the saucepan. Heat on medium for about 5 minutes, stirring occasionally, until hot. Serves 4.

1 serving: 60 Calories; 0.2 g Total Fat (0 g Mono, 0.1 g Poly, 0 g Sat); 0 mg Cholesterol; 14 g Carbohydrate; 3 g Fibre; 1 g Protein; 732 mg Sodium

Pictured on page 30.

RABBIT'S GARDEN SOUP: After blending, add 1 to 2 cups (250 to 500 mL) of frozen mixed vegetables to the soup in the saucepan. Heat on medium for 5 to 7 minutes, stirring occasionally, until the vegetables are tender and the soup is bubbling.

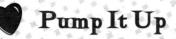

Top: Rabbit's Soup, page 29
Bottom: Mexi-Taters, page 31

Mexi-Taters

A meatless Mexican meal in minutes!
(Say that three times!) The veggie
ground round gives you the protein.

Get It Together: fork, oven mitts, sharp knife, cutting board, teaspoon, medium bowl, measuring spoons, dry measures, grater, mixing spoon, microwave-safe plate

1. Large unpeeled potato	1	1
2. Salsa	2 tbsp.	30 mL
Sour cream	2 tbsp.	30 mL
3. Veggie ground round, lightly packed	1/2 cup	125 mL
4. Grated jalapeño Monterey Jack cheese	1/4 cup	60 mL

1. Poke the fork into the potato in several places. Microwave on high (100%) for 3 minutes. Use the oven mitts to turn the potato over. Microwave for another 3 minutes. The potato is cooked when you can easily poke it with a fork. Let the potato stand for about 5 minutes until cool enough to handle. Cut the potato in half lengthwise. Use the teaspoon to scoop the potato flesh from both halves into the bowl. Leave a little bit of the potato flesh attached to the skins so they don't tear. Place the potato skins on the plate. Set aside. Mash the potato flesh in the bowl with the fork.

2. Add the salsa and sour cream to the bowl. Stir until well mixed.

3. Add the veggie ground round. Stir. Spoon the potato mixture into the potato skins.

4. Sprinkle with the cheese. Microwave, covered, on high (100%) for about 2 minutes until the cheese is melted. Serves 2.

1 serving: 224 Calories; 6.9 g Total Fat (1.9 g Mono, 0.4 g Poly, 4.2 g Sat); 19 mg Cholesterol; 25 g Carbohydrate; 2 g Fibre; 17 g Protein; 412 mg Sodium

Pictured on page 30.

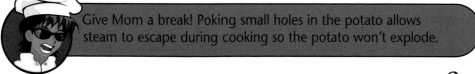

Give Mom a break! Poking small holes in the potato allows steam to escape during cooking so the potato won't explode.

What did the **baby corn** ask the **mom corn?**
Where's Pop Corn?

Chop Chop Suey

You'll devour this colourful, quick chop suey in a heartbeat—unless you need practice with chopsticks! Great over leftover rice, sprinkled with soy sauce for more Asian flavour.

Get It Together: sharp knife, cutting board, vegetable peeler, measuring spoons, dry measures, can opener, strainer, large frying pan, mixing spoon

1. Cooking oil	1 tsp.	5 mL
Small broccoli florets	1 cup	250 mL
Sliced fresh white mushrooms	1 cup	250 mL
2. Fresh bean sprouts	3 cups	750 mL
Can of sliced water chestnuts, drained and chopped	8 oz.	227 mL
Grated peeled carrot	1/2 cup	125 mL
3. Sweet and sour sauce	2 tbsp.	30 mL
Sliced green onion	1 tbsp.	15 mL

1. Heat the cooking oil in the frying pan on medium-high for 2 minutes. Add the broccoli and mushrooms. Cook for about 2 minutes, stirring often, until the vegetables start to soften.

2. Add the next 3 ingredients. Cook for about 2 minutes, stirring often, until hot.

3. Add the sauce. Stir until the vegetables are coated. Sprinkle with the green onion. Serves 2.

1 serving: 175 Calories; 3 g Total Fat (1.4 g Mono, 0.9 g Poly, 0.3 g Sat); 0 mg Cholesterol; 33 g Carbohydrate; 6 g Fibre; 8 g Protein; 91 mg Sodium

Pictured on page 33.

Bright Idea: Chop some tofu, cooked chicken or beef and add it with the bean sprouts. An extra dash of sauce will give your protein a nice glaze.

An **eight-year-old** has an average heart rate of 9 0, while a 1 2-year-old's average heart rate is 8 5.

Chop Chop Suey, above

Piggy Bank Popcorn

*Compare the cost of store-bought microwave
popcorn to this recipe! Your piggy bank will get fat,
but your heart will be happy.*

Get It Together: small microwave-safe cup, measuring spoons, small bowl, mixing spoon, brown paper lunch bag, medium bowl

1. Butter	1 tbsp.	15 mL
2. Unpopped corn	2 tbsp.	30 mL
Cooking oil	1/8 tsp.	0.5 mL
Seasoned salt	1/2 tsp.	2 mL

1. Put the butter into the cup. Microwave, covered, on high (100%) for about 10 seconds until melted. Set aside.

2. Put the corn into the small bowl. Add the cooking oil. Stir until coated. Transfer the corn to the paper bag. Close the bag by making 2 tight folds, about 1/2 inch (12 mm) each, at the top of the bag. Microwave, folded-side down, on high (100%) for 1 1/2 to 2 minutes until the popping slows to about 1 second between pops. Carefully open the bag and pour the popcorn into the medium bowl. Drizzle with the butter. Sprinkle with the seasoned salt. Toss until coated. Serves 1.

1 serving: 152 Calories; 9.4 g Total Fat (2.8 g Mono, 0.9 g Poly, 5 g Sat); 21 mg Cholesterol; 16 g Carbohydrate; 3.27 g Fibre; 2 g Protein; 680 mg Sodium

Pictured on page 35.

Bright Idea: There's no end to the popabilities! Use Cajun, Tex-Mex or barbecue seasoning. Or try a sprinkle of grated Parmesan or Cheddar cheese.

Pineapple Fizz

*Friends will think you have a heart of gold if
you offer them this creamy, fizzy drink.*

Get It Together: can opener, tablespoon, blender, liquid measures, dry measures, 4 large glasses, teaspoon

1. Tropical fruit juice	2 cups	500 mL
Can of crushed pineapple (with juice)	14 oz.	398 mL
Vanilla frozen yogurt	1 cup	250 mL
2. Ginger ale	1 cup	250 mL

1. Put the first 3 ingredients into the blender. Cover with the lid. Process until smooth. Pour into the glasses.

2. Add 1/4 cup (60 mL) ginger ale to each glass. Stir gently. Serves 4.

1 serving: *218 Calories; 1.4 g Total Fat (0.4 g Mono, 0.1 g Poly, 0.8 g Sat); 3 mg Cholesterol; 50 g Carbohydrate; 1 g Fibre; 4 g Protein; 44 mg Sodium*

Pictured below.

Bright Idea: Mix and match different juices with other soft drinks such as orange or lemon lime to create new flavours.

Increase the cool factor of this drink by chillling the pineapple and ginger ale in the fridge before making it.

Top: Pineapple Fizz, page 34
Bottom: Piggy Bank Popcorn, page 34

Plushie

Pump up your cool factor with this frosty, pale orange ice-crystal slush. Scoop it into paper cups or fun bowls for a refreshing treat.

Get It Together: can opener, strainer, 2 cup (500 mL) microwave-safe liquid measure, mixing spoon, blender, 8 x 8 inch (20 x 20 cm) pan, plastic wrap

1. Cans of crushed pineapple (with juice),   2   2
    14 oz., (398 mL), each

2. Box of peach jelly powder   3 oz.   85 g

1. Drain enough juice from the pineapple to make 1 cup (250 mL) in the measuring cup. Set aside the pineapple and the rest of the juice. Microwave the measured juice on high (100%) for 1 to 2 minutes until small bubbles form.

2. Add the jelly powder. Stir for about 1 minute until dissolved. Carefully pour the mixture into the blender. Add the crushed pineapple and remaining juice. Cover with the lid. Process until smooth. Pour the mixture into the pan. Cover with the plastic wrap. Freeze overnight until firm. Let stand at room temperature for 30 minutes before serving. Serves 8.

1 serving: 89 Calories; 0.1 g Total Fat (0 g Mono, 0 g Poly, 0 g Sat); 0 mg Cholesterol; 22 g Carbohydrate; 1 g Fibre; 1 g Protein; 28 mg Sodium

Pictured on page 37.

Banana Berry "Ice Cream"

You can try other fruit for this creamy, rich dessert, but don't omit the ripe bananas—they're the secret ingredient! Have a heart and share with your kid brother or sister.

Get It Together: sharp knife, cutting board, dry measures, food processor (not blender!)

1. Frozen medium bananas,   2   2
    page 103, sliced
    Frozen mixed berries   1 cup   250 mL

(continued on next page)

1. Put the banana slices and berries into the food processor. Pulse with an on/off motion until the fruit is finely chopped. Process for about 1 minute until smooth. Serves 2.

1 serving: 147 Calories; 0.9 g Total Fat (0.1 g Mono, 0.2 g Poly, 0.2 g Sat); 0 mg Cholesterol; 37 g Carbohydrate; 5 g Fibre; 2 g Protein; 2 mg Sodium

Pictured below.

If there's any left over, you can keep it in an airtight container in the freezer for up to a week. Let it soften on the counter for 15 minutes before you scoop it.

What do you call two birds in love?
Tweethearts!

Top left: Banana Berry "Ice Cream", page 36   Bottom right: Plushie, page 36

Fuel Your Think Tank
Breakfasts and Healthy Fats for Your Brain

If your heart is the pump that makes your body function, your brain is the control system. It keeps you breathing and takes care of your body temperature, blood pressure and heart rate. It also helps you sort out all the information coming at your senses while you're awake.

On top of that, your brain uses your nerves to automatically tell your body parts how to move, so you can walk AND chew gum without even thinking about it. Positively mind-boggling!

Finally, your brain lets you think, imagine and feel emotions (*hmmm ... if I don't clean up this messy kitchen before Mom gets home, she'll ground me and I'll be really upset. Where's the dishcloth?*). Pretty sophisticated stuff for an organ the size of a small head of cauliflower!

One of the best ways to get your think tank fuelled up is to have a good breakfast. Math quiz tomorrow? Get some brain food into you before you leave the house!

Another way to nourish your brain is to eat foods rich in healthy fats. You'll find these in fish, nuts, seeds and peanut butter. Other "smart" choices include bananas, peas, eggs, broccoli and tofu, made with soybeans. Try our mind-bending recipes for brain-boosting nutrients.

Broken-Hearted Egg Toast

Broken-Hearted Egg Toast

All you eggheads out there will get a kick out of designing this breakfast. Think fast! What other shapes can you make with the cookie cutters at your place?

Get It Together: measuring spoons, table knife, 3 inch (7.5 cm) heart-shaped cookie cutter, medium frying pan, cooking spray, fork, pancake lifter, dinner plate

1. Softened butter   2 tsp.   10 mL
   Whole wheat bread slice   1   1

2. Large egg   1   1

3. Salt, sprinkle
   Pepper, sprinkle

1. Spread the butter on both sides of the bread. Cut a heart shape from the centre of the bread with the cookie cutter.

2. Grease the frying pan with the cooking spray. Heat the pan on medium for 3 minutes. Put the bread slice and cut-out in the pan beside each other. Carefully break the egg into the hole in the bread slice. Break the yolk by poking it with the fork.

3. Sprinkle the egg with salt and pepper. Cook for about 4 minutes until the egg is almost set and the bread is golden. Carefully turn over the bread slice and the cut-out with the lifter. Cook for another 1 to 2 minutes until the bottoms are golden and the egg is set. Remove to the plate. Tear the cut-out in half to make a "broken heart." Place both halves beside the egg toast on the plate. Serves 1.

1 serving: 213 Calories; 14 g Total Fat (4.6 g Mono, 1.3 g Poly, 6.7 g Sat); 237 mg Cholesterol; 14 g Carbohydrate; 2 g Fibre; 9 g Protein; 292 mg Sodium

Pictured on page 38.

The cut-out may cook faster than the egg toast. Keep an eye on it! Turn it over as soon as the first side is golden, and put it on the plate as soon as both sides are done.

Nut And Honey Granola

*A granola fit for whiz kids. Have a bowl
with milk or yogurt for breakfast, or use with
Banana Monkey Crunch, page 22. Store in
an airtight container for up to three weeks.*

Get It Together: dry measures, 2 large bowls, small saucepan, mixing spoon,
measuring spoons, 2 baking sheets with sides, oven mitts, sharp knife, cutting board

1.			
Large flake rolled oats	3 cups	750 mL
Chopped walnuts	1/2 cup	125 mL
Raw sunflower seeds	1/2 cup	125 mL
Sesame seeds	1/4 cup	60 mL
Sliced almonds	1/4 cup	60 mL
Wheat germ	1/4 cup	60 mL
2. Liquid honey	1/3 cup	75 mL
Cooking oil	1/4 cup	60 mL
Brown sugar, packed	2 tbsp.	30 mL
Ground cinnamon	1 tsp.	5 mL
Vanilla extract	1 tsp.	5 mL
3. Finely chopped dried apricot	1/2 cup	125 mL
Medium sweetened coconut	1/4 cup	60 mL

1. Place 1 oven rack in the centre position and the other rack in the lower
position. Turn the oven on to 300°F (150°C). Put the first 6 ingredients into
1 of the bowls. Stir until well mixed.

2. Put the next 5 ingredients into the saucepan. Heat on medium for about
2 minutes, stirring constantly, until the brown sugar is dissolved. Carefully
drizzle over the rolled oat mixture. Stir until coated. Spread on both
ungreased baking sheets. Bake on separate racks for 10 minutes, stirring
occasionally. Carefully switch the positions of the baking sheets. Bake for
another 10 to 15 minutes, stirring occasionally, until golden. Remove the
baking sheets. Turn the oven off. Transfer the granola mixture to the
other bowl.

3. Add the apricot and coconut. Stir well. Cool. Makes about 6 cups (1.5 L).

*1/2 cup (125 mL): 319 Calories; 16.4 g Total Fat (6.1 g Mono, 7.3 g Poly, 2 g Sat); 0 mg Cholesterol;
38 g Carbohydrate; 5 g Fibre; 9 g Protein; 9 mg Sodium*

Pictured on page 41.

40 **Fuel Your Think Tank**

Nut And Honey Granola, page 40

Smart Shake

A no-brainer on mornings when a science test looms!
A slice of toast makes this a complete breakfast.
Pack along leftovers for a lunchtime treat.

Get It Together: sharp knife, cutting board, blender, dry measures, liquid measures

1.			
Caramel dessert tofu		1/2 cup	125 mL
Frozen medium banana, page 103, sliced		1	1
Milk		1 cup	250 mL
Chopped pitted dates		1/4 cup	60 mL

1. Put all 4 ingredients into the blender. Cover with the lid. Process for about 1 minute until smooth. Serves 1.

1 serving: 489 Calories; 10.6 g Total Fat (2.4 g Mono, 4.2 g Poly, 2.9 g Sat); 11 mg Cholesterol; 85 g Carbohydrate; 7 g Fibre; 23 g Protein; 214 mg Sodium

Pictured on page 42.

Bright Idea: Instead of using caramel tofu and dates, try peach tofu with peach-applesauce, or berry tofu with fresh or frozen blueberries.

 Fuel Your Think Tank

Bottom: Smart Shake, page 41
Top: Frittata Muffins, page 43

Frittata Muffins

You get an A+ for knowing that the combination of bacon, cheese and vegetables in this egg-packed breakfast can double as a lunch. Freeze extras and microwave frozen muffins for a minute on busy days.

Get It Together: muffin pan, cooking spray, grater, dry measures, measuring spoons, medium bowl, liquid measures, mixing spoon, blender, oven mitts, wire rack, table knife

1.			
Grated medium Cheddar cheese	1 cup	250 mL
Grated unpeeled zucchini	1 cup	250 mL
Frozen peas	1 cup	250 mL
Frozen kernel corn	1 cup	250 mL
Real bacon bits	2 tbsp.	30 mL
2. Large eggs	8	8
Biscuit mix	1/2 cup	125 mL
Milk	1/2 cup	125 mL
Salt	1/4 tsp.	1 mL
Pepper	1/4 tsp.	1 mL

1. Place the oven rack in the centre position. Turn the oven on to 350°F (175°C). Grease the muffin cups with the cooking spray. Put the first 5 ingredients into the bowl. Stir until well mixed. Spoon the vegetable mixture into the muffin cups until 3/4 full.

2. Carefully break the eggs into the blender. Add the remaining 4 ingredients. Cover with the lid. Process until smooth. Pour over the vegetable mixture in the muffin cups until full. Bake for about 30 minutes until the muffins are golden and set. Remove the pan to the wire rack. Let the muffins stand for 5 minutes. Turn the oven off. Run the knife around the muffins to loosen them. Remove them to the wire rack to cool. Makes 12 muffins. Serves 6.

1 serving: 260 Calories; 14.3 g Total Fat (4.7 g Mono, 1.8 g Poly, 5.8 g Sat); 304 mg Cholesterol; 16 g Carbohydrate; 2 g Fibre; 16 g Protein; 462 mg Sodium

Pictured on page 42.

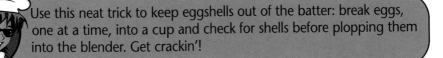

Use this neat trick to keep eggshells out of the batter: break eggs, one at a time, into a cup and check for shells before plopping them into the blender. Get crackin'!

Ocean Burgers

*You'll ace that report with these crunchy
potato cakes packed with salmon.*

Get It Together: medium bowl, fork, dry measures, can opener, measuring spoons, sharp knife, cutting board, mixing spoon, dinner plate, large frying pan, pancake lifter, table knife

1. Large egg	1	1
Leftover mashed potatoes	1 cup	250 mL
Can of skinless, boneless pink salmon, drained	6 oz.	170 g
Seasoned salt	1/4 tsp.	1 mL
Chopped fresh chives (or 1/4 tsp.,1 mL, dried)	1 tsp.	5 mL
2. Cornflake crumbs	1 cup	250 mL
3. Cooking oil	1 tbsp.	15 mL
4. Quick Tartar Sauce, page 45	4 tbsp.	60 mL
Whole wheat hamburger buns, split	4	4
Medium tomato, sliced	1	1
Shredded lettuce, lightly packed	1 cup	250 mL

1. Break the egg into the bowl. Beat the egg a little with the fork. Add the next 4 ingredients. Stir until well mixed.

2. Put 1/2 the cornflake crumbs on the plate. Set aside. Add the remaining crumbs to the fish mixture. Stir well. Divide the fish mixture into 4 equal portions. Shape portions into 1/2 inch (12 mm) thick patties. Gently press both sides of the patties into the crumbs on the plate until coated.

3. Heat the cooking oil in the frying pan on medium for 3 minutes. Add the patties. Cook for about 3 minutes until the bottoms are golden. Use the lifter to check. Turn the patties over. Cook for another 2 to 3 minutes until the bottoms are golden. Remove the pan from the heat.

4. Spread the tartar sauce on the buns. Top with the patties, tomato slices and lettuce. Serves 4.

1 serving: 410 Calories; 19.6 g Total Fat (9.3 g Mono, 5.6 g Poly, 3.6 g Sat); 72 mg Cholesterol; 49 g Carbohydrate; 1 g Fibre; 12 g Protein; 858 mg Sodium

Pictured on page 45.

(continued on next page)

QUICK TARTAR SAUCE: Put 1/4 cup (60 mL) mayonnaise, 1 tbsp. (15 mL) sweet pickle relish and 1/4 tsp. (1 mL) lemon juice into a small bowl. Stir well. Makes about 4 tbsp. (60 mL).

INDIAN OCEAN BURGERS (we dare ya!): Add 1/4 tsp. (1 mL) curry powder to the fish mixture before making the patties. Wrap the patties and toppings in naan bread instead of hamburger buns.

Brain teaser: What happens twice in a week, once in a year, but never in a day?

The letter "e".

Ocean Burger, page 44

Under-The-Sea Taco

*For a taste of the Mexican seaside, squeeze
fresh lime over your fish sticks before
you add the other toppings.*

Get It Together: baking sheet with sides, oven mitts, dinner plate, measuring spoons, dry measures, sharp knife, cutting board, table knife, grater

1. Fish sticks	3	3
2. Whole wheat flour tortilla (9 inch, 22 cm, diameter)	1	1
Sour cream	2 tbsp.	30 mL
Grated Monterey Jack cheese	2 tbsp.	30 mL
Shredded lettuce, lightly packed	1/4 cup	60 mL
Salsa	2 tbsp.	30 mL

1. Cook the fish sticks on the baking sheet according to the directions on the package. Set aside. Turn the oven off.

2. Place the tortilla on the plate. Spread the sour cream in the centre of the tortilla. Place the fish sticks, side by side, on the top 1/2 of the tortilla. The fish sticks should point to the top of the tortilla. Top them with the remaining 3 ingredients. Fold the bottom of the tortilla up over the filling. Fold the sides over the filling. Serves 1.

1 serving: 541 Calories; 23.2 g Total Fat (8.5 g Mono, 4.8 g Poly, 8.6 g Sat); 117 mg Cholesterol; 59 g Carbohydrate; 7 g Fibre; 23 g Protein; 966 mg Sodium

Pictured on page 47.

Bright Idea: Instead of using fish sticks, use 1 cooked fish fillet.

The **brain** of Albert Einstein weighed 1,230 grams or 2.7 **pounds**. The average **human brain** **weighs** 1,400 grams or 3 **pounds**.

Top: Seafood Chowder, page 49
Bottom: Under-The-Sea Taco, above

Top: Sun-Dried Tomato Dip, page 49
Bottom: Frozen Banana Rocket, page 50

Seafood Chowder

Invite a few other wise guys to sit down to this creamy chowder loaded with tasty seafood. You can find cooked shrimp in bulk at your grocer's seafood counter.

Get It Together: can opener, large saucepan, liquid measures, whisk, mixing spoon, dry measures, sharp knife, cutting board, measuring spoon

1.	Can of condensed cream of potato soup	10 oz.	284 mL
	Milk	2 cups	500 mL
2.	Frozen hash brown potatoes	1 cup	250 mL
	Cooked small shrimp	1 cup	250 mL
	Chopped imitation crabmeat	1 cup	250 mL
	Parsley flakes	1 tsp.	5 mL

1. Put the soup into the saucepan. Slowly add the milk, stirring constantly with the whisk until the mixture is smooth. Heat on medium for about 10 minutes, stirring occasionally, until the soup is steaming but not bubbling.

2. Add the remaining 4 ingredients. Stir. Cook for about 5 minutes, stirring occasionally, until the soup is bubbling. Serves 4.

1 serving: 222 Calories; 4.1 g Total Fat (0.9 g Mono, 0.9 g Poly, 1.9 g Sat); 91 mg Cholesterol; 27 g Carbohydrate; 1 g Fibre; 19 g Protein; 1091 mg Sodium

Pictured on page 47.

Sun-Dried Tomato Dip

Geniuses know they can refrigerate this in an airtight container for up to three days to serve with their favourite veggies. See page 106 for serving ideas.

Get It Together: dry measures, blender

1.	Package of soft tofu	10 1/2 oz.	300 g
	Grated Parmesan cheese	1/3 cup	75 mL
	Sun-dried tomato salad dressing	1/3 cup	75 mL

1. Put all 3 ingredients into the blender. Cover with the lid. Process until well combined. Makes about 1 cup (250 mL). Serves 4.

1 serving: 228 Calories; 20.5 g Total Fat (9.5 g Mono, 6.8 g Poly, 3.2 g Sat); 21 mg Cholesterol; 3 g Carbohydrate; 1 g Fibre; 10 g Protein; 511 mg Sodium

Pictured on page 48.

Frozen Banana Rocket

Need a brain-booster before you start that book report?
Get inspired with the flavours and textures of this snack—
crunchy on the outside, icy cold and sweet inside.

Get It Together: measuring spoons, small frying pan, mixing spoon, plastic wrap, sharp knife, wooden craft stick, cutting board, dinner plate

1. Chopped walnuts	2 tbsp.	30 mL
Raw sunflower seeds	1 tbsp.	15 mL
2. Medium banana	1	1
3. Vanilla yogurt	1 tbsp.	15 mL

1. Put the walnuts and sunflower seeds in the frying pan. Heat on medium for 3 to 5 minutes, stirring often, until golden. Remove the pan from the heat. Cool.

2. Trim 1/4 inch (6 mm) from 1 end of the banana. Insert the wooden craft stick into the trimmed end. Tear off a sheet of plastic wrap that is just a little longer than the banana. Place on the countertop. Sprinkle the walnut mixture over the plastic wrap.

3. Holding the stick with the banana over the plate, spoon the yogurt over the whole banana until coated. Place it on the walnut mixture. Turn the banana until coated. Wrap with the same sheet of plastic wrap. Freeze for about 2 hours until firm. Serves 1.

1 serving: 317 Calories; 19.4 g Total Fat (4 g Mono, 12.4 g Poly, 2 g Sat); 1 mg Cholesterol; 33 g Carbohydrate; 5 g Fibre; 9 g Protein; 13 mg Sodium

Pictured on page 48.

Bright Idea: Go nuts! Instead of walnuts, use chopped pecans or hazelnuts.

What did the little banana say to its mother when it didn't want to go to school?
I don't peel good!

Frosty Fruit Soup

*No brain freeze here—just terrific tastes
and a refreshing temperature.*

Get It Together: sharp knife, cutting board, dry measures, liquid measures, blender, soup bowl

1. Frozen chopped cantaloupe, page 103	1 cup	250 mL
Tropical fruit juice	3/4 cup	175 mL
Peach dessert tofu	1/3 cup	75 mL
2. Fresh (or frozen) blueberries	1/4 cup	60 mL

1. Put the first 3 ingredients into the blender. Cover with the lid. Process until smooth. Pour into the bowl.

2. Scatter the blueberries over top. Serves 1.

1 serving: 263 Calories; 4.9 g Total Fat (0.9 g Mono, 2.4 g Poly, 0.6 g Sat); 0 mg Cholesterol; 50 g Carbohydrate; 3 g Fibre; 9 g Protein; 26 mg Sodium

Pictured below.

Bright Idea: Out of blueberries? Use whatever chopped fresh or frozen fruit you find in the fridge or fruit bowl.

Why is orange juice so smart?
It concentrates.

Frosty Fruit Soup, above

Power Play
Protein for Your Muscles

The next time people tell you to sit down, be quiet, and not move a muscle, tell them it's impossible. You might be able to obey the first two orders, but the third? Forget about it! You can't make your heart stop beating, and it's a pretty important muscle.

It's one of more than 600 in your body, from the tiny muscles that make your eyelids quiver or form the goosebumps on your arms, to the biggest one (you're sitting on it—it's called the gluteus maximus, because maximus means, well, biggest). Some of your muscles act like elastic bands and connect to your bones to help make them move. If you want to kick a ball or arm-wrestle your pals, those elastic bands push and pull your body along.

Muscles need the amino acids from protein-rich foods to repair and rebuild. Meat, chicken, turkey, fish and eggs are high-protein foods. You can also find protein in dairy products, dried beans, nuts and seeds. If you're choosing proteins from plant sources, remember to combine them with grains to get all your amino acids. Peanut butter on whole wheat, and beans with rice, are great combinations.

Then go out and tussle with your muscles, 'cause the best way to make them bigger and stronger is to let them do what they want to do—exercise!

Big Breakfast

*Talk about a power play! This triple-protein combo
will make it easy to rev up your mornings.*

Get It Together: measuring spoons, table knife, sharp knife, cutting board,
microwave-safe soup bowl, dry measures, small cup, fork, liquid measures, grater

1. Ketchup	1 tbsp.	15 mL
Whole wheat bread slice	1	1
Chopped cooked ham	1/4 cup	60 mL
2. Large egg	1	1
Milk	1/4 cup	60 mL
Salt, sprinkle		
Pepper, sprinkle		
3. Grated medium Cheddar cheese	2 tbsp.	30 mL

1. Spread the ketchup on the bread. Cut the bread into strips about 1 inch
(2.5 cm) wide, then cut the strips into 1 inch (12 mm) pieces. Put the bread
into the bowl. Scatter the ham over the bread.

2. Break the egg into the cup. Beat with the fork until the egg is bubbly on top.
Add the next 3 ingredients. Beat until well mixed. Pour evenly over the ham.
Do not stir. Microwave, covered, on high (100%) for 2 to 3 minutes until the
centre of the egg mixture is set.

3. Sprinkle with the cheese. Microwave on high (100%) for another 10 to
15 seconds until the cheese is melted. Serves 1.

*1 serving: 287 Calories; 13.6 g Total Fat (4.9 g Mono, 1.4 g Poly, 5.9 g Sat); 252 mg Cholesterol;
22 g Carbohydrate; 2 g Fibre; 20 g Protein; 906 mg Sodium*

Pictured on page 52.

Bright Idea: Try salsa or barbecue sauce instead of ketchup. Leftover cooked
sausage or real bacon bits work in place of ham.

Make this the night before for a fast breakfast! Follow the recipe,
putting everything but the cheese in the bowl. Cover with plastic
wrap. Refrigerate overnight. In the morning, remove the plastic
wrap, and cook as directed. Don't forget the cheese!

Hakuna Frittata

*Prepare for a power surge with the egg
and cheese proteins in this fabulous frittata.
Makes enough to split with a sibling.*

Get It Together: measuring spoons, small non-stick frying pan with lid, dry measures, mixing spoon, small bowl, whisk, grater

1. Cooking oil	2 tsp.	10 mL
Frozen hash brown potatoes	1/2 cup	125 mL
2. Large eggs	2	2
Milk	2 tbsp.	30 mL
Salt, sprinkle		
Pepper, sprinkle		
3. Grated havarti cheese	1 cup	250 mL

1. Heat the cooking oil in the frying pan on medium for 3 minutes. Add the potatoes. Cook for about 5 minutes, stirring constantly, until golden brown. Turn down the heat to medium-low.

2. Break the eggs into the bowl. Add the next 3 ingredients. Beat with the whisk until the mixture is bubbly on top. Spread the potatoes evenly in the pan and pour the egg mixture evenly on top. Do not stir.

3. Sprinkle with the cheese. Do not stir. Cover with the lid. Cook for about 5 minutes until the cheese is melted and the egg is set. Serves 2.

1 serving: 370 Calories; 25.6 g Total Fat (8.9 g Mono, 2.6 g Poly, 12.1 g Sat); 277 mg Cholesterol; 12 g Carbohydrate; 1 g Fibre; 22 g Protein; 532 mg Sodium

Pictured on page 55.

Bright Idea: No havarti cheese? No worries! Use the cheese that's in the fridge. Cheddar's a good substitute.

Jaw muscles can provide about **91 kilograms** or **200 pounds** of force to bring the **back teeth** together for **chewing.**

Top: Corn Tomato Chowder, page 56
Bottom: Hakuna Frittata, above

Corn Tomato Chowder

*Powerfully hungry? This soup will hit the spot, especially
if there's leftover potato in the fridge. Pack the cheese
separately if you're bringing it for a school lunch.*

Get It Together: liquid measures, can opener, large saucepan, whisk, dry measures,
sharp knife, cutting board, ladle, 4 soup bowls, grater

1.	Can of condensed tomato soup	10 oz.	284 mL
	Milk	2 cups	500 mL
2.	Diced cooked potato	1 cup	250 mL
	Frozen kernel corn	1 cup	250 mL
	Chopped cooked ham	3/4 cup	175 mL
3.	Grated medium Cheddar cheese	1/2 cup	125 mL

1. Put the soup into the saucepan. Slowly add the milk, stirring constantly
with the whisk until the mixture is smooth.

2. Add the next 3 ingredients. Stir. Cook on medium for about 10 minutes,
stirring occasionally, until the vegetables are hot and the soup begins to boil.
Ladle into the bowls.

3. Sprinkle with the cheese. Serves 4.

*1 serving: 280 Calories; 10.5 g Total Fat (3.4 g Mono, 1.2 g Poly, 5.1 g Sat); 35 mg Cholesterol;
33 g Carbohydrate; 2 g Fibre; 16 g Protein; 1014 mg Sodium*

Pictured on page 55.

Fiesta Pizza

*You'll say "Olé!" when you try this crispy, thin-crust pizza
topped with zippy salsa, tender chicken and sweet corn.*

Get It Together: baking sheet with sides, dry measures, tablespoon, sharp knife,
cutting board, can opener, strainer, grater, oven mitts, wire rack

1.	Flour tortilla (9 inch, 22 cm, diameter)	1	1
	Salsa	1/4 cup	60 mL
2.	Chopped cooked chicken	1/3 cup	75 mL
	Canned kernel corn, drained	1/4 cup	60 mL
	Grated jalapeño Monterey Jack cheese	1/2 cup	125 mL

(continued on next page)

1. Place the oven rack in the centre position. Turn the oven on to 425°F (220°C). Place the tortilla on the baking sheet. Use the back of the spoon to spread the salsa on the tortilla.

2. Scatter the chicken and corn on top of the salsa. Sprinkle with the cheese. Bake for about 10 minutes until the cheese is melted and bubbling. Remove the baking sheet to the wire rack. Let stand for 5 minutes. Turn the oven off. Serves 1.

1 serving: 549 Calories; 23.8 g Total Fat (7.6 g Mono, 3.3 g Poly, 11.3 g Sat); 89 mg Cholesterol; 50 g Carbohydrate; 4 g Fibre; 34 g Protein; 948 mg Sodium

Pictured below.

Bright Idea: You can use frozen kernel corn, thawed, instead of canned corn.

What's the strongest vegetable in the world?
A muscle sprout.

Fiesta Pizza, page 56

Budding Chef's Salad

Learning how to boil an egg is a basic cooking skill.
Drizzle this salad with your favourite dressing.

Get It Together: small saucepan. tablespoon. small bowl. sharp knife. cutting board. dry measures. grater. medium bowl

1. Large egg		1	1
Cold water			
2. Chopped or torn green leaf lettuce, lightly packed		1 cup	250 mL
Julienned deli ham slices		1/3 cup	75 mL
Julienned deli turkey breast slices		1/3 cup	75 mL
Grated medium Cheddar cheese		1/2 cup	125 mL

1. Put the egg into the saucepan. Add enough cold water to cover the egg. Cook, covered, on medium-high until the water is bubbling. Turn down the heat to medium-low. Cook, covered, for another 10 minutes. Remove the pan from the heat. Carefully remove the egg with the tablespoon to the small bowl. Cover the egg with cold water and keep changing the water until the egg is cool. Peel the egg. Cut it lengthwise into quarters.

2. Put the lettuce into the medium bowl. Scatter the next 3 ingredients over the lettuce. Arrange the egg quarters on the salad around the edge of the bowl. Serves 1.

1 serving: 451 Calories; 27.3 g Total Fat (9.2 g Mono, 2.3 g Poly, 13.2 g Sat); 349 mg Cholesterol; 5 g Carbohydrate; 1 g Fibre; 45 g Protein; 1123 mg Sodium

Pictured on page 58.

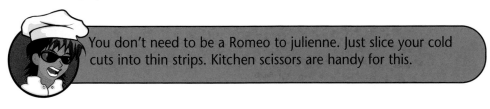

You don't need to be a Romeo to julienne. Just slice your cold cuts into thin strips. Kitchen scissors are handy for this.

Goosebumps happen when the little arrector muscle at the base of each hair pulls the hair upright.

Top: Budding Chef's Salad, above
Bottom: Cheesy Lunch Lasagne, page 60

Cheesy Lunch Lasagne

This meatless muscle-booster makes enough to refrigerate in airtight containers for school lunches.

Get It Together: medium bowl, liquid measures, dry measures, mixing spoon, 9 inch (22 cm) deep dish pie plate, cooking spray, grater, baking sheet, oven mitts, wire rack

1.		
Thick tomato pasta sauce	1 1/2 cups	375 mL
Veggie ground round, lightly packed	1 cup	250 mL
Cottage cheese	1 cup	250 mL

2.		
Thick tomato pasta sauce	1/2 cup	125 mL

3.		
Flour tortillas (9 inch, 22 cm, diameter)	4	4
Grated mozzarella cheese	1 3/4 cups	425 mL

1. Place the oven rack in the centre position. Turn the oven on to 375°F (190°C). Put the first 3 ingredients into the bowl. Stir well.

2. Grease the pie plate with the cooking spray. Spread the second amount of pasta sauce in the pie plate.

3. To assemble the lasagne, spread or layer ingredients in the pie plate as follows:

   a) 1 tortilla
   b) 3/4 cup (175 mL) cottage cheese mixture
   c) 1/3 cup (75 mL) mozzarella cheese

Repeat steps a), b) and c) until all the ingredients are used—remember, you will have extra mozzarella to use on the top layer. Put the pie plate on the baking sheet. Bake, uncovered, for about 45 minutes until the cheese is melted and just starting to brown. Remove the lasagne to the wire rack. Let stand for 10 minutes. Turn the oven off. Serves 6.

1 serving: 395 Calories; 15.5 g Total Fat (5.9 g Mono, 2.7 g Poly, 6.1 g Sat); 30 mg Cholesterol; 42 g Carbohydrate; 3 g Fibre; 22 g Protein; 1074 mg Sodium

Pictured on page 58.

It takes **more than 30 muscles** to **frown** and about **16 to smile.**

Thousand On A Raft

Beans are a powerful protein source. Dress up this barge o' beans with a drizzle of molasses, or a squirt of ketchup or mustard.

Get It Together: can opener, dry measures, small microwave-safe bowl, oven mitts, mixing spoon, dinner plate

1.	Canned baked beans in tomato sauce	1/2 cup	125 mL
2.	Whole wheat bread slice	1	1

1. Put the beans into the bowl. Microwave, covered, on high (100%) for 30 seconds. Stir. Microwave, covered, for about 30 seconds more until hot. Remove the bowl from the microwave. Cover to keep warm.

2. Toast the bread slice. Place on the plate. Spoon the beans on top. Serves 1.

1 serving: 195 Calories; 1.8 g Total Fat (0.5 g Mono, 0.5g Poly, 0.4 g Sat); 0 mg Cholesterol; 41 g Carbohydrate; 12 g Fibre; 9 g Protein; 682 mg Sodium

Pictured below.

Bright Idea: Add a blanket of good taste to warm up the thousand! Top this sandwich with your favourite cheese slices and microwave on high (100%) for a few seconds until melted.

Give those beans a good stir before you spoon them out, so you get an even amount of beans and sauce.

Thousand On A Raft, above

Egg Drop Soup, below

Egg Drop Soup

This Asian soup is egg-zactly what you need on a chilly day before you head off to after-school activities. A dash of soy sauce and a sprinkle of chopped green onion are extra flavour boosters.

Get It Together: liquid measures, small saucepan, dry measures, mixing spoon, fork

1. Chicken broth	1 1/2 cups	375 mL
Frozen peas	1/4 cup	60 mL
2. Large egg	1	1

1. Put the broth into the saucepan. Heat on medium until bubbling. Add the peas. Stir.

2. Break the egg into the liquid measure. Beat the egg just a little with the fork. Slowly pour the egg in a thin stream into the bubbling soup, stirring constantly. The egg will cook immediately. Serves 1.

1 serving: 166 Calories; 7.2 g Total Fat (2.9 g Mono, 1.2 g Poly, 2.2 g Sat); 217 mg Cholesterol; 7 g Carbohydrate; 2 g Fibre; 17 g Protein; 1354 mg Sodium

Pictured above.

Tofu Taco Dip

*You can ramp up the heat factor by choosing
a spicier salsa. Perfect as a raw veggie dip, you
can also pair it with A Yotta Yams, page 104.*

Get It Together: measuring spoons, blender, airtight container

1. Package of soft tofu	10 1/2 oz.	300 g
Salsa	2 tbsp.	30 mL
Taco seasoning mix, stir before measuring	1 tbsp.	15 mL

1. Put all 3 ingredients into the blender. Cover with the lid. Process until smooth. Transfer the dip to the airtight container. Chill for 1 hour before serving. Makes about 1 1/3 cups (325 mL). Serves 4.

*1 serving: 69 Calories; 4 g Total Fat (0.9 g Mono, 2.2 g Poly, 0.6 g Sat); 0 mg Cholesterol;
4 g Carbohydrate; 1 g Fibre; 6 g Protein; 229 mg Sodium*

Pictured below.

You can keep this dip in the fridge for up to 3 days so you can have a snack as soon as you get home from school.

Tofu Taco Dip, above

Muchos Nachos

*After the game, your teammates will
muscle right in on this great snack. Baked chips,
veggie ground round and vegetables make
this popular snack extra healthy.*

Get It Together: foil, baking sheet with sides, cooking spray, sharp knife, cutting board, dry measures, measuring spoons, oven mitts, wire rack

1.			
Bag of baked corn tortilla chips	10 1/2 oz.	300 g
Package of veggie ground round	3/4 lb.	340 g
Chopped red pepper	1 cup	250 mL
Package of grated Mexican cheese blend	14 oz.	400 g
2. Medium tomatoes, chopped	2	2
Sliced green onion	2 tbsp.	30 mL

1. Place the oven rack in the centre position. Turn the oven on to 375°F (190°C). Cover the baking sheet with the foil. Grease with the cooking spray. To assemble your nachos, layer ingredients on the baking sheet as follows:

   a) 4 cups (1 L) tortilla chips
   b) 2/3 cup (150 mL) veggie ground round
   c) 1/3 cup (75 mL) red pepper
   d) 1 cup (250 mL) of the cheese

   Repeat steps a), b), c) and d) until all the ingredients are used—remember, you will have extra cheese to use on the top layer. Bake for about 15 minutes until the cheese is melted and starting to brown. Remove the baking sheet to the wire rack. Turn the oven off.

2. Sprinkle nachos with the tomato and green onion. Serves 8.

1 serving: 342 Calories; 17.7 g Total Fat (5 g Mono, 1 g Poly, 10.7 g Sat); 52 mg Cholesterol; 24 g Carbohydrate; 3 g Fibre; 23 g Protein; 580 mg Sodium

Pictured on page 65.

MUCHOS NACHOS FOR ONE: Craving nachos but the team's not here? No problem! Spread about 2 cups (500 mL) tortilla chips on a microwave-safe dinner plate. Top with 1/4 cup (60 mL) veggie ground round, 1/4 cup (60 mL) chopped red pepper and 1/3 cup (75 mL) grated Cheddar cheese. Microwave on high (100%) for 1 to 2 minutes until the cheese is melted. Top with some chopped tomato and sliced green onion.

Muchos Nachos, above

The Ins & Outs of Eating
Fibre for Your Digestion

They say that what goes up must come down. It's the same with what goes in, especially when it comes to your body. At the centre of the in/out process is your digestive system. That's where the pizza slice you had for lunch gets broken down, and the important nutrients are sent off to different parts of your body.

Fibre keeps your digestive tract healthy, making sure that the food you eat doesn't hang around for too long. It's way easier to make a dash for third base or leap across a dance floor if you don't feel like there's a bowling ball in your stomach.

High-fibre foods tend to be lower in fat, which is good for your heart. And because fibre is bulky, it makes you feel full longer, helping to fight off those mid-morning munchies.

Look for breads, bagels and tortillas made with whole wheat. Check out the fibre content on your cereal box—the bigger the number the higher the fibre content. Fruit and vegetables, including dried fruit, have fibre; so do baked beans and brown rice. They're all designed to keep you moving!

Quick Fruit Crisp

Quick Fruit Crisp

*This will warm up your insides on a cold morning.
Or serve with ice cream as a dessert. Now that's easy
to swallow! You can use our granola recipe on page 40.*

Get It Together: dry measures, measuring spoons, microwave-safe soup bowl,
soup spoon, oven mitts

1.	Frozen mixed berries	1/2 cup	125 mL
	Fruit salad snack cup, drained	4 oz.	112 mL
	Diced peaches snack cup, drained	4 oz.	112 mL
	Liquid honey	1 tsp.	5 mL
2.	Cornstarch	1 tsp.	5 mL
3.	Granola	1/2 cup	125 mL

1. Put the first 4 ingredients into the bowl. Stir until the fruit is coated
with the honey.

2. Sprinkle the cornstarch over the fruit mixture. Stir until well mixed.

3. Sprinkle the granola over the fruit mixture. Do not stir. Microwave, covered,
on high (100%) for 3 to 4 minutes until the sauce is bubbling along the edge
of the bowl. Serves 1.

*1 serving: 477 Calories; 18.2 g Total Fat (5 g Mono, 9.3 g Poly, 3.1 g Sat); 0 mg Cholesterol;
77 g Carbohydrate; 11 g Fibre; 10 g Protein; 16 mg Sodium*

Pictured on page 66.

Bright Idea: The juice from the snack cups is too good to waste! Drain the juice
into a large glass and top with orange juice for a special morning punch. Or add
a splash of sparkling water for a fizzy drink.

Do you suffer from **borborygmus**
(pronounced "bore-ber-IG-mas") at school?
No, it's not a **boring math class**.
It's the sound of a **rumbling tummy**.

Weekend Wake-Up Call

Perfect for a morning-after breakfast with your sleepover friends—"pick up the phone" to chat about last night's Truth or Dare game! Remember to cut the banana in half lengthwise.

Get It Together: dinner plate, measuring spoons, table knife, dry measures, sharp knife, cutting board

1. Whole wheat bread slice	1	1
Berry spreadable cream cheese	3 tbsp.	50 mL
2. Peanut butter	2 tbsp.	30 mL
3. Fresh raspberries	1/4 cup	60 mL
4. Medium banana	1/2	1/2
5. Shoestring licorice (about 18 inches, 45 cm, length)	1	1

1. Toast the bread. Place it on the plate. Spread it with the cream cheese.

2. Spread the peanut butter over the cream cheese in a square on the bottom of the toast, leaving about 1/3 of the cream cheese uncovered on the top (see photo).

3. Arrange the raspberries, stem-end down, on top of the peanut butter to make the buttons of the telephone dial pad.

4. Put the banana half near the top of the toast for the handset. Decorate with any leftover raspberries.

5. Insert 1 end of the licorice into 1 end of the banana. Insert the other end into the side of the toast. Serves 1.

1 serving: 505 Calories; 33.8 g Total Fat (12.8 g Mono, 5.6 g Poly, 13.5 g Sat); 49 mg Cholesterol; 42 g Carbohydrate; 6 g Fibre; 15 g Protein; 447 mg Sodium

Pictured on page 69.

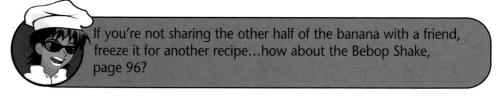

If you're not sharing the other half of the banana with a friend, freeze it for another recipe...how about the Bebop Shake, page 96?

Weekend Wake-Up Call, above

Breakfast Split

Dessert for breakfast—does it get any better than this? Have your backpack ready so you can "split" as soon as you're done with breakfast.

Get It Together: dry measures, ice cream scoop, dessert bowl, cutting board, sharp knife

1. Vanilla frozen yogurt	3/4 cup	175 mL
2. Medium banana	1	1
3. Fresh raspberries	1/4 cup	60 mL
Chopped fresh strawberries	1/4 cup	60 mL
Granola	1/4 cup	60 mL

1. Put the frozen yogurt into the bowl.

2. Cut the banana in half crosswise. Cut both halves lengthwise into 2 pieces, for a total of 4 pieces. Arrange around the frozen yogurt in the bowl.

3. Sprinkle with the berries and granola. Serves 1.

1 serving: 472 Calories; 13.4 g Total Fat (3.6 g Mono, 5 g Poly, 4.2 g Sat); 11 mg Cholesterol; 82 g Carbohydrate; 7 g Fibre; 14 g Protein; 117 mg Sodium

Pictured on front cover and on page 71.

Bright Idea: What's your favourite fresh or canned fruit? Use that instead of the berries.

Hawaiian Toasts

Mini Hawaiian pizzas! Add the drained pineapple juice to a glass of orange juice for extra tropical taste.

Get It Together: baking sheet with sides, cooking spray, measuring spoons, table knife, grater, dry measures, oven mitts, wire rack

1. Whole wheat English muffin, split	1	1
Pizza sauce	2 tbsp.	30 mL
2. Deli turkey breast slices	2	2
Diced pineapple snack cup, drained	5 oz.	142 mL
Grated havarti cheese	1/2 cup	125 mL

(continued on next page)

1. Place the oven rack in the centre position. Turn the oven on to 400°F (205°C). Grease the baking sheet with the cooking spray. Place the English muffin halves, cut-side up, on the baking sheet. Spread them with the pizza sauce.

2. Cover the pizza sauce with the turkey slices. Fold them if necessary to fit the muffin. Top with the pineapple pieces. Sprinkle with the cheese. Bake for 10 to 15 minutes until the cheese is melted and bubbling. Turn the oven off. Remove the baking sheet to the wire rack. Let stand for 2 minutes. Serves 1.

1 serving: 544 Calories; 20.8 g Total Fat (5.9 g Mono, 2.1 g Poly, 11.2 g Sat); 144 mg Cholesterol; 44 g Carbohydrate; 6 g Fibre; 47 g Protein; 1085 mg Sodium

Pictured below.

Top: Breakfast Split, page 70
Bottom: Hawaiian Toasts, page 70

Nutty Noodles

*We've used peanut butter instead of the instant
noodle flavour packet for this dish for a good boost
of protein and fibre! Now that's using your noodle!*

Get It Together: small microwave-safe bowl, liquid measures, oven mitts,
medium microwave-safe bowl, mixing spoons, strainer, measuring spoons,
dry measures

1. Package of instant noodles (keep flavour packet for another use)	3 oz.	85 g
Baby carrots	6	6
Water	1 cup	250 mL
2. Water	1/4 cup	60 mL
Peanut butter	2 tbsp.	30 mL
Teriyaki sauce	2 tbsp.	30 mL
Sesame oil (optional)	1/2 tsp.	2 mL
Ground ginger	1/4 tsp.	1 mL
3. Frozen peas	1/4 cup	60 mL
4. Dry-roasted peanuts	1 tbsp.	15 mL

1. Break the noodles into large chunks and put them into the small bowl. Add
the carrots. Pour the first amount of water over top. Microwave, covered, on
high (100%) for 3 minutes. Let stand, covered, for about 3 minutes until the
noodles are softened. Use the strainer to drain the noodle mixture. Return
the noodle mixture to the bowl. Cover to keep warm. Set aside.

2. Put the next 5 ingredients into the medium bowl. Stir until well mixed.
Microwave, covered, on high (100%) for about 15 seconds until hot.

3. Add the peas. Stir. Add the noodle mixture. Toss with the mixing spoons
until coated.

4. Sprinkle with the peanuts. Serves 1.

*1 serving: 668 Calories; 25.2 g Total Fat (11.3 g Mono, 7.1 g Poly, 4.8 g Sat); 81 mg Cholesterol;
88 g Carbohydrate; 9 g Fibre; 27 g Protein; 1642 mg Sodium*

Pictured on page 72.

Where did the vegetables go for a drink?
The salad bar.

Top: Nutty Noodles, above
Bottom: Beany Burrito, page 74

Beany Burrito

The word "burrito" comes from the Spanish word burro, *which means donkey. This little donkey delivers lots of high-fibre beans right to you.*

Get It Together: microwave-safe plate. can opener. small spoon. dry measures. grater. sharp knife. cutting board

1. Flour tortilla (9 inch, 22 cm, diameter)   1   1
Canned baked beans in tomato sauce   1/2 cup   125 mL
  (see tip, page 61)

2. Grated medium Cheddar cheese   1/4 cup   60 mL
Chopped cooked roast beef   1/4 cup   60 mL

1. Place the tortilla on the plate. Spread the beans evenly on the tortilla almost to the edge.

2. Scatter the cheese and beef on top of the beans. Fold the sides over the filling. Roll up tightly from the bottom to trap the beans. Microwave, uncovered, on high (100%) for about 1 minute until hot. Serves 1.

1 serving: 477 Calories; 14 g Total Fat (4.6 g Mono, 2.3 g Poly, 5.9 g Sat); 45 mg Cholesterol; 63 g Carbohydrate; 12 g Fibre; 27 g Protein; 992 mg Sodium

Pictured on page 72.

Mexi-Bean Dip

Not only are beans and pumpkin seeds good for your innards, but they're a great protein combination. This tastes terrific cold, so save any leftovers for a school lunch.

Get It Together: dry measures. microwave-safe soup bowl. tablespoon. microwave-safe dinner plate. oven mitts. grater

1. Canned refried beans   1/2 cup   125 mL
Salsa   1/2 cup   125 mL
Grated medium Cheddar cheese   1/2 cup   125 mL

2. Salted, roasted shelled pumpkin seeds   1/4 cup   60 mL
Tortilla chips   24   24

(continued on next page)

1. Put the beans into the bowl. Use the back of the spoon to spread them evenly on the bottom of the bowl. Spread the salsa on the beans. Sprinkle with the cheese. Microwave, covered, on high (100%) for about 2 1/2 minutes until the beans are bubbling along the edge of the bowl. Place the bowl on the plate.

2. Sprinkle the pumpkin seeds on top of the cheese. Arrange the tortilla chips on the plate around the bowl. Microwave on high (100%) for 30 seconds to warm the chips. Serves 2.

1 serving: 464 Calories; 29.3 g Total Fat (10.5 g Mono, 7.1 g Poly, 10.1 g Sat); 37 mg Cholesterol; 32 g Carbohydrate; 10 g Fibre; 23 g Protein; 850 mg Sodium

Pictured below.

BEAN QUESADILLA SANDWICHES: Forget the chips and spread the heated dip on 2 flour tortillas instead. Sprinkle with the seeds and roll them up.

HOT BEAN POCKETS: Spoon the heated dip into mini pita pockets and add the seeds..

An **appestat** (pronounced "APPi-stat") is like a thermostat for your appetite. It's in your brain and tells you when **you're hungry** or full.

Mexi-Bean Dip, page 74

Almond Berry Trifle

A fabulous way to trifle with fibre. You'd never guess you'd put bread in this pudding—it tastes like cake!

Get It Together: dry measures, small frying pan, small plate, mixing spoon, small microwave-safe bowl, oven mitts, sharp knife, cutting board, large drinking glass, small spoon

1. Slivered almonds	2 tbsp.	30 mL
2. Frozen mixed berries	1 1/2 cups	375 mL
Whole wheat bread slice, chopped	1	1
Vanilla pudding snack cup	3 1/2 oz.	99 g

1. Put the almonds into the frying pan. Heat them on medium for 3 to 5 minutes, stirring often, until golden. Transfer the almonds to the plate. Cool.

2. Put the berries into the bowl. Microwave, covered, on high (100%) for 1 1/2 minutes. Put 1/3 of the bread into the glass. Spoon 1/3 of the berries with the juice on top of the bread. Spoon 1/3 of the pudding on top of the berries. Repeat 2 more times until the berries, bread and pudding are layered in the glass. Sprinkle with the almonds. Serves 1.

1 serving: 433 Calories; 15.6 g Total Fat (7.7 g Mono, 2.6 g Poly, 3.8 g Sat); 17 mg Cholesterol; 67 g Carbohydrate; 12 g Fibre; 12 g Protein; 274 mg Sodium

Pictured on page 79.

Coconut Crisps

Who knew fibre could taste so good? Refrigerate these in an airtight container for up to one week. (Bet they'll be gone before that!)

Get It Together: dry measures, medium saucepan, sharp knife, cutting board, measuring spoons, mixing spoon, dinner plate, serving plate

1. Butter	1/4 cup	60 mL
2. Chopped pitted dates	1 cup	250 mL
Water	2 tbsp.	30 mL
3. Crisp rice cereal	1/2 cup	125 mL
Raw sunflower seeds	1/2 cup	125 mL
4. Medium unsweetened coconut	1/3 cup	75 mL

(continued on next page)

1. Melt the butter in the saucepan on medium.

2. Add the dates and water. Cook, stirring constantly, until the mixture is bubbling. Turn down the heat to low. Cook for about 3 minutes, stirring constantly, until the mixture is thick. Remove the pan from the heat. Cool for 10 minutes.

3. Add the cereal and sunflower seeds. Stir well.

4. Put the coconut onto the plate. Using a 1 tbsp. (15 mL) measure, drop the date mixture onto the coconut. Roll the mixture in the coconut until coated. Roll coconut crisps between your hands to make balls. Arrange on the serving platter. Chill in the refrigerator until firm. Makes 15 crisps.

3 crisps: 303 Calories; 21.6 g Total Fat (4.4 g Mono, 5.4 g Poly, 10.5 g Sat); 26 mg Cholesterol; 27 g Carbohydrate; 5 g Fibre; 5 g Protein; 133 mg Sodium

Pictured below.

W hy did the banana go out with the prune?
Because he couldn't find a date.

Coconut Crisps, page 76

Cranberry Almond Chewies

Wrap these squares and pop them into the freezer for up to one month. They'll be easy to grab for school lunch desserts too.

Get It Together: dry measures, small frying pan, mixing spoon, large bowl, 9 x 9 inch (22 x 22 cm) pan, cooking spray, small saucepan, measuring spoons, wooden spoon, sharp knife

1. Sliced almonds	1/2 cup	125 mL
2. Cornflakes cereal	8 cups	2 L
Dried cranberries	2 cups	500 mL
3. Butter	1/4 cup	60 mL
Golden corn syrup	2/3 cup	150 mL
Brown sugar, packed	1/2 cup	125 mL
Vanilla extract	1/4 tsp.	1 mL

1. Put the almonds into the frying pan. Heat on medium for 3 to 5 minutes, stirring often, until golden. Remove the pan from the heat. Transfer the almonds to the bowl. Cool.

2. Add the cereal and cranberries. Stir. Set aside.

3. Grease the pan with the cooking spray. Set aside. Put the butter into the saucepan. Heat on medium until melted. Add the corn syrup and brown sugar. Stir. Cook for about 2 minutes, stirring constantly, until the mixture is bubbling. Remove the saucepan from the heat. Add the vanilla extract. Stir well. Pour over the cereal mixture in the bowl. Stir with the wooden spoon until coated. Press the cereal mixture firmly into the pan. Let stand until cooled completely. Makes 16 chewies.

1 chewy: 216 Calories; 5.1 g Total Fat (2.1 g Mono, 0.5 g Poly, 2.1 g Sat); 8 mg Cholesterol; 43 g Carbohydrate; 5 g Fibre; 2 g Protein; 182 mg Sodium

Pictured on page 79.

Got yourself in a sticky situation? Use a wooden spoon for "no-bake" treats. Sticky mixtures don't cling to wood as easily as they stick to metal. Another good trick: spray your hands with cooking spray or use a piece of greased waxed paper to press the mixture into the pan.

Top right: Almond Berry Trifle, page 76
Bottom: Cranberry Almond Chewies, page 78

Go with the Flow
Iron and B Vitamins for Your Blood

Just under your skin, a river of life pulses through a super-pipeline of blood vessels. Without blood, your body would stop working. You'd never grow and nothing would ever heal.

Your blood works like a delivery service, picking up oxygen from your heart and nutrients from the food you've eaten and depositing them all over your body. On its way back to the heart, your blood collects the used oxygen—now carbon dioxide—and delivers it to your lungs for you to breathe out. It takes about a minute for a blood cell to zip from your heart to your toes.

Your blood needs iron-rich food to do its job properly. Without iron, you start to feel tired and sluggish; you can't even be bothered to chase after your kid sister when she takes the last cookie, let alone be a star on the playing field or in the school play. Some of the B vitamins, such as B6, B12 and folic acid, are also important for blood.

Iron-rich food includes beef, pork, chicken, fish, baked beans, whole grains, dried fruit and eggs. Combine these with dark green vegetables for a real iron punch. Look for B vitamins in vegetables, fruit, fish, chickpeas and pinto beans.

Cheesy Potato Scramble

Cheesy Potato Scramble

You artery-ly (ought to really!) try this hash brown potato breakfast. Add a splash of ketchup to the veggies if you want some wake-up tang.

Get It Together: measuring spoons, small non-stick frying pan with lid, dry measures, mixing spoon, small microwave-safe bowl, grater

1. Cooking oil		1 tsp.	5 mL
Frozen hash brown potatoes		3/4 cup	175 mL
2. Frozen Italian mixed vegetables		3/4 cup	175 mL
3. Grated mozzarella cheese		1/2 cup	125 mL

1. Heat the cooking oil in the frying pan on medium-high for 2 minutes. Add the potatoes. Cook for about 4 minutes, stirring occasionally, until golden brown. Turn down the heat to medium-low.

2. Put the vegetables into the bowl. Microwave, covered, on high (100%) for about 90 seconds until thawed. Add to the potatoes. Cook for 3 minutes, stirring constantly.

3. Sprinkle with the cheese. Do not stir. Cover with the lid. Cook for about 2 minutes until the cheese is melted. Serves 1.

1 serving: *438 Calories; 19.3 g Total Fat (6.8 g Mono, 2.4 g Poly, 8.8 g Sat); 49 mg Cholesterol; 50 g Carbohydrate; 7 g Fibre; 20 g Protein; 319 mg Sodium*

Pictured on page 80.

Bright Idea: Any kind of frozen vegetables or leftover cooked vegetables will work for this recipe. You don't need to microwave leftover vegetables first. Just add them to the potatoes and they'll heat in the pan.

If you strung your **blood vessels end to end**, they'd go around the globe **2.5** times.

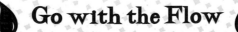

Nutty Monkey

You'll go ape for this icy milkshake. A medium banana gives you almost one-quarter of your vitamin B6 needs, and it tastes so good!

Get It Together: liquid measures, measuring spoons, blender

1. Frozen medium banana, page 103	1	1
Milk	1/2 cup	125 mL
Chocolate milk	1/2 cup	125 mL
Peanut butter	2 tbsp.	30 mL

1. Put all 4 ingredients into the blender. Cover with the lid. Process for about 30 seconds until smooth. Serves 1.

1 serving: 437 Calories; 22 g Total Fat (9.6 g Mono, 5 g Poly, 6.2 g Sat); 14 mg Cholesterol; 48 g Carbohydrate; 4 g Fibre; 18 g Protein; 305 mg Sodium

Pictured on page 85.

Bright Idea: To make this drink taste more like a smoothie, use a fresh banana instead of a frozen one.

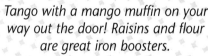

Apple Mango Muffins

Tango with a mango muffin on your way out the door! Raisins and flour are great iron boosters.

Get It Together: muffin pan, cooking spray, dry measures, small saucepan, vegetable peeler, cutting board, sharp knife, 2 large bowls, fork, mixing spoon, measuring spoons, wooden toothpick, oven mitts, wire rack

1. Butter	1/2 cup	125 mL
2. Large egg	1	1
Medium apples, peeled and chopped	2	2
Frozen mango pieces, thawed, page 103	1 1/2 cups	375 mL
Raisins	1 cup	250 mL
Unsweetened applesauce	1 cup	250 mL

(continued on next page)

3. All-purpose flour	3 cups	750 mL
Brown sugar, packed	1 cup	250 mL
Baking soda	1 tsp.	5 mL
Salt	1/2 tsp.	2 mL

1. Place the oven rack in the centre position. Turn the oven on to 375°F (190°C). Grease the muffin cups with the cooking spray. Set aside. Melt the butter in the saucepan on medium. Set aside.

2. Break the egg into 1 of the large bowls. Beat with the fork until the egg is bubbly on top. Add the next 4 ingredients. Stir until well mixed. Add the butter. Mix well.

3. Put the remaining 4 ingredients into the other large bowl. Stir well. Dig a hole in the centre of the flour mixture with the mixing spoon. Put the fruit mixture into the hole. Stir just until the flour mixture is moistened. Spoon the batter into the muffin cups. The cups will be full and the batter mounded. Bake for 30 to 35 minutes until the pick inserted straight down into the centre of a muffin comes out clean. Turn the oven off. Remove the pan to the wire rack. Let stand for 5 minutes. Remove the muffins to the wire rack to cool. Makes 12 muffins.

1 muffin: 345 Calories; 9 g Total Fat (2.6 g Mono, 0.6 g Poly, 5.3 g Sat); 40 mg Cholesterol; 64 g Carbohydrate; 3 g Fibre; 5 g Protein; 304 mg Sodium

Pictured on page 85.

It's always a good idea to check your baking for doneness at the earlier time given in a recipe, because you don't want your baking to dry out. If there's still wet batter on your toothpick, bake for another 5 minutes and test again with another pick.

W hat's the name of the **blood specialist's boat?**
The **Blood Vessel.**

Chicken Pockets

*Do chickens have pockets? I guess they must,
otherwise where would they put their chicken
fingers? Plump up your pita with this filling
filling—colourful, crunchy and delicious!*

Get It Together: sharp knife, cutting board, dry measures, medium bowl, mixing spoons, measuring spoons

1. Chopped fresh spinach leaves, stems removed, lightly packed	1 cup	250 mL
Chopped cooked chicken	1/2 cup	125 mL
Chopped unpeeled English cucumber	1/4 cup	60 mL
Chopped tomato	1/4 cup	60 mL
2. Ranch dressing	2 tbsp.	30 mL
Salt, sprinkle		
Pepper, sprinkle		
3. Pita bread (7 inch, 18 cm, diameter), halved	1	1

1. Put the first 4 ingredients into the bowl. Toss.

2. Add the next 3 ingredients. Toss until coated.

3. Spoon into the pita pockets. Makes 2 pockets. Serves 1.

1 serving: 536 Calories; 25.8 g Total Fat (7.1 g Mono, 12.6 g Poly, 5 g Sat); 85 mg Cholesterol; 41 g Carbohydrate; 3 g Fibre; 34 g Protein; 714 mg Sodium

Pictured on page 85.

Bright Idea: Instead of spinach, use your favourite salad greens. Creamy Caesar dressing is a tasty alternative to ranch dressing.

The average adult has at least 4 litres or 16 cups of blood—enough to fit into a big milk jug!

Clockwise from top left:
Apple Mango Muffins, page 82
Nutty Monkey, page 82
Chicken Pockets, above

Peanut Butter Wedgies

*Double this recipe and give your big brother
or sister a wedgie or two. Want a more
colourful wedgie? Add a few dried, chopped
apricots and some raisins to the banana.*

Get It Together: measuring spoons, table knife, sharp knife, cutting board

1. Peanut butter	2 tbsp.	30 mL
Flour tortilla (9 inch, 22 cm, diameter)	1	1
2. Medium banana, sliced	1	1

1. Spread the peanut butter on the tortilla.

2. Arrange the banana slices on half of the tortilla. Fold the tortilla in half to cover the banana slices. Press down lightly. Cut into 4 wedges. Serves 1.

1 serving: 506 Calories; 21.4 g Total Fat (9.6 g Mono, 6.6 g Poly, 4.1 g Sat); 0 mg Cholesterol; 70 g Carbohydrate; 6 g Fibre; 15g Protein; 466 mg Sodium

Pictured on page 87.

Bright Idea: When you just don't feel like a wedgie, forget about slicing the banana. Put the whole thing on the peanut butter and roll the tortilla up around it to form a wrap.

Cheesy Meatball Macaroni

*Beef up leftover mac and cheese with saucy
meatballs and pump up your iron. Add a
simple salad to balance your meal.*

Get It Together: dry measures, 2 microwave-safe soup bowls, measuring spoons, tablespoon

1. Leftover macaroni and cheese	1/2 cup	125 mL
Water	1 tsp.	5 mL
2. Frozen cooked meatballs,	3	3
Tomato pasta sauce	1/4 cup	60 mL
3. Process Cheddar cheese slice	1	1

(continued on next page)

1. Put the macaroni into 1 of the bowls. Sprinkle with the water. Dig a hole in the macaroni with the tablespoon.

2. Put the meatballs into the other bowl. Microwave, covered, on high (100%) for 30 to 45 seconds until thawed. Place the meatballs in the hole in the macaroni. Spoon the sauce onto the meatballs. Microwave, covered, on high (100%) for about 90 seconds until the meatballs are hot.

3. Place the cheese on top of the meatballs. Microwave, covered, on high (100%) for about 15 seconds until the cheese is melted. Serves 1.

1 serving: 445 Calories; 19.4 g Total Fat (3.5 g Mono, 1.1 g Poly, 4.6 g Sat); 20 mg Cholesterol; 27 g Carbohydrate; 1 g Fibre; 17 g Protein; 1608 mg Sodium

Pictured below.

Top: Cheesy Meatball Macaroni, page 86
Bottom: Peanut Butter Wedgies, page 86

Top: Monster Pudding Pops, page 90
Bottom: Healthy Chocolate Chippers,
page 89

Healthy Chocolate Chippers

*We've added rolled oats and dried apricot to
our famous Chocolate Chippers recipe—can you
feel your blood racing already?*

Get It Together: cookie sheets, cooking spray, large bowl, dry measures, mixing
spoon, measuring spoons, small bowl, sharp knife, cutting board, teaspoon, oven mitts,
wire racks

1.	Softened butter	1/2 cup	125 mL
	Brown sugar, packed	3/4 cup	175 mL
	Large egg	1	1
	Vanilla extract	1/2 tsp.	2 mL
2.	All-purpose flour	3/4 cup	175 mL
	Cornstarch	2 tbsp.	30 mL
	Baking soda	1/2 tsp.	2 mL
	Salt	1/4 tsp.	1 mL
3.	Quick-cooking rolled oats	1 cup	250 mL
	Chopped dried apricot	3/4 cup	175 mL
	Chocolate chips	3/4 cup	175 mL

1. Place the oven rack in the centre position. Turn the oven on to 350°F
(175°C). Grease the cookie sheets with the cooking spray. Set aside. Put the
butter and brown sugar into the large bowl. Mix until smooth and creamy.
Add the egg. Stir well. Add the vanilla extract. Stir until smooth.

2. Put the next 4 ingredients into the small bowl. Stir. Add about 1/2 of the
flour mixture to the butter mixture. Stir well. Add the rest of the flour
mixture. Stir until no dry flour remains.

3. Add the remaining 3 ingredients. Stir well. Drop the dough by heaping
teaspoons onto the cookie sheets about 2 inches (5 cm) apart. Bake 1 cookie
sheet at a time for 10 to 15 minutes until the cookies are golden. Remove
each cookie sheet to a wire rack. Let stand for 5 minutes. Turn the oven off.
Transfer the cookies to the wire racks to cool. Makes about 24 cookies.

*4 cookies: 420 Calories; 19 g Total Fat (5.7 g Mono, 1.1 g Poly, 11 g Sat); 63 mg Cholesterol;
60 g Carbohydrate; 3 g Fibre; 6 g Protein; 311 mg Sodium*

Pictured on front cover and on page 88.

CHEWY FRUIT COOKIES: For an even healthier snack, use raisins or dried
cranberries instead of the chocolate chips.

Monster Pudding Pops

This pudding treat studded with fruit goes into the freezer, but it won't make your blood run cold!

Get It Together: liquid measures, blender, sharp knife, cutting board, dry measures, dinner plate, 4 paper cups (5 oz., 142 mL, size), 4 wooden craft sticks, plastic wrap

1. Milk	2 cups	500 mL
Box of instant vanilla pudding powder	1	1
(4 serving size)		
2. Chopped dried apricot	1/2 cup	125 mL
Dried cranberries	1/4 cup	60 mL
Raisins	1/4 cup	60 mL

1. Put the milk and pudding powder into the blender. Cover with the lid. Process for about 2 minutes until smooth.

2. Add the remaining 3 ingredients. Pulse with an on/off motion until the fruit is well chopped. Pour the pudding mixture into the paper cups until full. Insert 1 stick into the middle of each cup. Set the cups on the plate. Cover loosely with the plastic wrap. Freeze overnight until firm. To loosen, run the bottom of each cup under hot water for 3 to 4 seconds. While holding the stick, push from the bottom of the cup to remove the pudding pop. Serves 4.

1 serving: 243 Calories; 1.7 g Total Fat (0.5 g Mono, 0.2 g Poly, 0.9 g Sat); 5 mg Cholesterol; 55 g Carbohydrate; 3 g Fibre; 5 g Protein; 436 mg Sodium

Pictured on page 88.

Bright Idea: Skip the freezing and pour the pudding mixture into dessert bowls. Don't forget the spoons!

Why did the doctor give up medicine and go into acting?

It was in her blood.

Nutty Fruit Bars

*Mush up ooey-gooey peanut butter and
banana first, then add all the chewy stuff.
As much fun to make as it is to eat!*

Get It Together: baking sheet, cooking spray, large bowl, fork, sharp knife, cutting board, mixing spoon, measuring spoons, dry measures, oven mitts, wire rack

1. Medium bananas, sliced	2	2
Peanut butter	3 tbsp.	50 mL
2. Quick-cooking rolled oats	3/4 cup	175 mL
Chopped dried apricot	1/4 cup	60 mL
Dried cranberries	1/4 cup	60 mL
Chopped pecans	1/4 cup	60 mL

1. Place the oven rack in the centre position. Turn the oven on to 350°F (175°C). Grease the baking sheet with the cooking spray. Put the banana slices in the bowl. Mash with the fork until smooth. Add the peanut butter. Stir until well mixed.

2. Add the remaining 4 ingredients. Stir well. Use a 1/4 cup (60 mL) measure to divide the mixture into 6 equal portions. Roll portions into 4 inch (10 cm) long logs. Press logs down to 1/2 inch (12 mm) thickness. Arrange them on the baking sheet. Bake for about 20 minutes until the edges are golden. Remove the baking sheet to the wire rack to cool. Turn the oven off. Serves 6.

1 serving: 191 Calories; 8.8 g Total Fat (4.5 g Mono, 2.4 g Poly, 1.4 g Sat); 0 mg Cholesterol; 26 g Carbohydrate; 4 g Fibre; 5 g Protein; 40 mg Sodium

Pictured on page 93.

NUTTY FRUIT COOKIES: Roll the dough into balls, using about 2 tbsp. (30 mL) for each cookie. Arrange on the baking sheet evenly spaced apart. Press cookies down to 1/2 inch (12 mm) thickness. Bake for about 20 minutes until golden. Remove the baking sheet to the wire rack to cool. Turn the oven off.

What's bright red and dumb?
A blood clod.

Enchanted Forest

You might not see the forest for these broccoli "trees," but you'll love the creamy hummus dip they stand in. Fresh and tasty.

Get It Together: measuring spoon, small plate, table knife, dry measures

1.	Vegetable spreadable cream cheese	2 tbsp.	30 mL
	Hummus	1/4 cup	60 mL
2.	Broccoli florets	1 cup	250 mL

1. Spread the cream cheese on the plate. Spread the hummus on the cream cheese.

2. Arrange the broccoli, stem-side down, in the hummus mixture to make a "forest." Serves 2.

1 serving: 174 Calories; 11.1 g Total Fat (4.8 g Mono, 1.6 g Poly, 4 g Sat); 16 mg Cholesterol; 13 g Carbohydrate; 3 g Fibre; 7 g Protein; 152 mg Sodium

Pictured on page 93.

Let It Flow with H₂O!

You are a breathing bag of water. About 70 per cent of you, including your muscles, lungs, brains and blood, is made up of H_2O. It regulates body temperature, protects joints and organs, and flushes away waste.

It makes sense to keep your body topped up with water long before you start to feel thirsty. Now, unless you're training for the Sahara Desert Death Race, good ol' H_2O will keep your body hydrated. Soft drinks are great as treats, but not at halftime or between periods! Here are a few ideas to make sure you're well-watered:

> Keep a pitcher of water in the fridge as a thirst-quencher.

> Pop a half-full water bottle into the freezer the night before a game, then top it with fresh water before you leave.

> Add a few mint sprigs or lemon slices to your next glass of water.

> A splash of apple or orange juice in hot water makes a great afternoon "tea."

> Try some water before a snack. Sometimes it's thirst your body is signalling, not hunger.

Top: Enchanted Forest, page 92
Bottom: Nutty Fruit Bars, page 91

The Cover Story
Vitamins A and C for Your Skin and Hair

Centuries ago, sailors looked a little scary after long voyages. They had dry hair that split and fell out, while their skin was rough, scaly, and easily bruised—signs of a disease called scurvy. The British navy finally ordered their sailors to eat fresh fruit and vegetables, especially limes. This stopped the scurvy and gave British sailors a new nickname: Limeys.

These days, it's easy to find enough vitamins A and C for great skin and hair. Your skin needs lots; it's your biggest organ. If you stretched an adult's skin flat, it would cover the top of a double bed and weigh about four kilograms or nine pounds. Some "skinny" blanket!

By the time you're an adult, you'll have the same amount of hair as a gorilla—about five million shafts growing everywhere except on your lips, the palms of your hands and the soles of your feet. The only difference? Human hair is much thinner than a gorilla's! Hair and nails are made of the same stuff as feathers, horses' hooves and the claws of your dog or cat.

For a great cover, look for vitamin C in citrus fruit, berries, tomatoes, peppers and potatoes. You'll find beta carotene, which helps you make vitamin A, in orange and dark green vegetables, such as carrots, pumpkin, sweet potatoes, apricots, broccoli and spinach. Vitamin A also helps you see well. It's true—have you ever seen a rabbit with glasses?

Square Roots

*The roots of your hair will love these root vegetables.
No worries if you can't chop up perfect squares—well,
cubes if you're thinking 3D—this isn't math class! Add
a scrambled egg to the pan for fast protein.*

Get It Together: fork, oven mitts, cutting board, sharp knife, measuring spoons,
medium frying pan, mixing spoon

1. Small unpeeled potato	1	1
Small unpeeled yam (or sweet potato)	1	1
2. Butter	1 tbsp.	15 mL
Cooking oil	1 tsp.	5 mL
3. Chili powder	1/2 tsp.	2 mL
Salt, sprinkle		
Pepper, sprinkle		

1. Poke the fork into the potato and yam in several places. Microwave on high
(100%) for 3 minutes. Use the oven mitts to turn them over. Microwave for
another 3 minutes. The potato and yam are cooked when you can easily poke
them with the fork. Let them stand for about 5 minutes until cool enough to
handle. Cut them into cubes.

2. Heat the butter and cooking oil in the frying pan on medium-high until the
butter is melted. Add the potato and yam. Stir.

3. Sprinkle with the remaining 3 ingredients. Cook for about 5 minutes, stirring
often, until the potato and yam cubes are browned around the edges and the
mixture is hot. Serves 2.

1 serving: 348 Calories; 8.6 g Total Fat (3.1 g Mono, 1.1 g Poly, 3.9 g Sat); 16 mg Cholesterol;
64 g Carbohydrate; 9 g Fibre; 5 g Protein; 88 mg Sodium

Pictured on page 94.

Most animals can make their own vitamin C.
Humans, other primates and guinea pigs
have lost this ability.

Bebop Shake

You'll be boppin' 'round the kitchen when you get a taste of this thick, creamy shake! Round out your breakfast with toast and a scrambled egg.

Get It Together: liquid measures, blender

1. Frozen medium banana, page 103	1/2	1/2
Orange juice	1 cup	250 mL
Diced peaches snack cup (with juice)	4 oz.	112 mL

1. Put all 3 ingredients into the blender. Cover with the lid. Process for about 30 seconds until smooth. Serves 1.

1 serving: 222 Calories; 0.8 g Total Fat (0.1 g Mono, 0.2 g Poly, 0.2 g Sat); 0 mg Cholesterol; 54 g Carbohydrate; 2 g Fibre; 3 g Protein; 8 mg Sodium

Pictured on page 99.

Veggie Potato Cakes

The skinny on these golden potato cakes? Get Mom or Dad to make extra mashed potatoes and carrots for dinner so you can make these the next morning.

Get It Together: medium bowl, fork, sharp knife, cutting board, dry measures, measuring spoons, 2 dinner plates, large frying pan, pancake lifter

1. Large egg	1	1
2. Leftover mashed potatoes	1 cup	250 mL
Finely chopped cooked carrot	1/2 cup	125 mL
Chopped fresh chives	1 tsp.	5 mL
(or 1/4 tsp.,1 mL, dried)		
Seasoned salt	1/4 tsp.	1 mL
3. Cornflake crumbs	1 cup	250 mL
4. Cooking oil	1 tbsp.	15 mL

(continued on next page)

1. Break the egg into the bowl. Beat with the fork until the egg is bubbly on top.

2. Add the next 4 ingredients. Stir well.

3. Put 1/2 the crumbs on 1 of the plates. Set aside. Add the rest of the crumbs to the potato mixture. Stir well. Divide the potato mixture into 6 equal portions. Shape portions into 1/2 inch (12 mm) thick patties. Gently press both sides of the patties into the crumbs on the plate until coated.

4. Heat the cooking oil in the frying pan on medium for 3 minutes. Add the patties. Cook for about 2 minutes until the bottoms are golden. Use the lifter to check. Turn the patties over. Cook for another 2 to 3 minutes until the bottoms are golden. Makes 6 potato cakes. Serves 2.

1 serving: 427 Calories; 14.3 g Total Fat (7 g Mono, 3.8 g Poly, 2.4 g Sat); 110 mg Cholesterol; 66 g Carbohydrate; 5 g Fibre; 9 g Protein; 1028 mg Sodium

Pictured on page 99.

Bright Idea: For a spicier breakfast, add a dash of curry powder to the potato mixture before making the patties.

Here's an awesome trick for making same-sized patties: line a 1/3 cup (75 mL) dry measure with plastic wrap. Fill the cup with potato mixture and press it down so it's level. Turn it onto a dinner plate to get the potato mixture out. Press down on the plastic wrap until the patty is about 1/2 inch (12 mm) thick. Use the same piece of plastic wrap to make the rest of the patties.

A kid walked into a store and asked for a potato clock. "I'm not sure what you mean," said the puzzled clerk. "Well," said the kid. "My teacher said I'd get to school on time if I got a potato clock." (Say it slowly: If I got up at eight o'clock...)

Asian Lettuce Wrap

Stop stumbling around in the dark—eat more carrots!
This wrap is a little messy to munch on, but you'll
love the delicious gingery taste.

Get It Together: small bowl, measuring spoons, mixing spoon, vegetable peeler, grater, dry measures, dinner plate

1. Mayonnaise   2 tbsp.   30 mL
   Soy sauce   1 tsp.   5 mL
   Ground ginger, sprinkle

2. Grated peeled carrot   1/4 cup   60 mL
   Fresh bean sprouts   1/4 cup   60 mL

3. Large green leaf lettuce leaf   1   1

1. Put the first 3 ingredients into the bowl. Stir until well mixed.

2. Add the carrot and bean sprouts. Stir until coated.

3. Place the lettuce leaf on the plate. Spoon the vegetable mixture in a horizontal line across the middle of the lettuce leaf. Fold the sides over the filling. Roll up from the bottom to enclose the filling. Serves 1.

1 serving: 231 Calories; 22.6 g Total Fat (12.5 g Mono, 7.5 g Poly, 2.2 g Sat); 17 mg Cholesterol; 6 g Carbohydrate; 1 g Fibre; 2 g Protein; 506 mg Sodium

Pictured on page 99.

Bright Idea: Stir 1 tsp. (5 mL) peanut butter in with the mayonnaise mixture for a flavourful protein boost. A few spoonfuls of leftover rice or noodles make this a well-rounded lunch.

What do you say to rotten lettuce? You should have your head examined!

Top: Bebop Shake, page 96
Centre: Veggie Potato Cakes, page 96
Bottom: Asian Lettuce Wrap, above

Waldorf Salad

*The creamy vanilla yogurt makes this a
salad that'll be hair today, gone tomorrow!
A muffin rounds this lunch out nicely.*

Get It Together: medium bowl, sharp knife, cutting board, dry measures, mixing spoon

1. Red medium unpeeled apple, chopped | 1 | 1
   Vanilla yogurt | 3/4 cup | 175 mL
   Seedless red grapes, halved | 3/4 cup | 175 mL
   Chopped celery | 1/2 cup | 125 mL
   Chopped pecans | 1/4 cup | 60 mL

1. Put all 5 ingredients into the bowl. Stir until the fruit is coated. Serves 2.

*1 serving: 262 Calories; 12.8 g Total Fat (7.1 g Mono, 2.8 g Poly, 2.1 g Sat); 5 mg Cholesterol;
36 g Carbohydrate; 3 g Fibre; 6 g Protein; 84 mg Sodium*

Pictured on page 102.

Hawaiian Coleslaw

*Crunchy coleslaw with a Hawaiian twist.
Try this in the Quick Hawaiian Rice Bowl on the
next page for a deliciously sweet hot lunch.*

Get It Together: large bowl, measuring spoons, mixing spoon, sharp knife, cutting board, dry measures, can opener

1. Mayonnaise | 3 tbsp. | 50 mL
   Sweet pickle relish | 1 1/2 tbsp. | 25 mL
   Teriyaki sauce | 1 tbsp. | 15 mL

2. Coleslaw mix | 4 cups | 1 L
   Chopped deli ham | 1 cup | 250 mL
   Canned pineapple tidbits, drained | 3/4 cup | 175 mL

(continued on next page)

1. Put the first 3 ingredients into the bowl. Stir until well mixed.

2. Add the remaining 3 ingredients. Stir until coated. Serves 3.

1 serving: 254 Calories; 16.9 g Total Fat (8.8 g Mono, 4.5 g Poly, 2.8 g Sat); 37 mg Cholesterol; 16 g Carbohydrate; 2 g Fibre; 11 g Protein; 1044 mg Sodium

Pictured below.

QUICK HAWAIIAN RICE BOWL: Place 1/2 cup (125 mL) leftover rice in a microwave-safe soup bowl. Add 1 cup (250 mL) Hawaiian Coleslaw. Microwave, covered, on high (100%) for 1 minute. Stir. Microwave for another 30 to 60 seconds until hot.

The reason for fingerprints?
So you have traction to pick up smooth objects.

Hawaiian Coleslaw, page 100

Top: Waldorf Salad, page 100
Bottom: Use Your Noodle Salad, page 103

Use Your Noodle Salad

*Chow mein noodles add extra crispness to the
crunchy veggies and bacon. The benefits
of this salad are more than skin deep!*

Get It Together: dry measures, medium bowl, sharp knife, cutting board,
vegetable peeler, grater, measuring spoons, mixing spoons

1.			
Chopped or torn romaine lettuce, lightly packed	1 cup	250 mL
Snow peas, trimmed and chopped	12	12
Thinly sliced unpeeled English cucumber	1/4 cup	60 mL
Grated peeled carrot	2 tbsp.	30 mL
Real bacon bits	1 tbsp.	15 mL
Ranch dressing	1 tbsp.	15 mL

2. Dry chow mein noodles   1/4 cup   60 mL

1. Put the first 5 ingredients into the bowl. Drizzle with the dressing. Use the
mixing spoons to toss until coated.

2. Sprinkle with the noodles. Serves 1.

*1 serving: 187 Calories; 10.7 g Total Fat (4 g Mono, 4.1 g Poly, 1 g Sat); 4 mg Cholesterol;
16 g Carbohydrate; 3 g Fibre; 5 g Protein; 219 mg Sodium*

Pictured on page 102.

How do you fix a broken tomato? Tomato paste!

Frosty Fruit Fun

Chop melons, apples and ripe bananas into bite-sized chunks and freeze in
single layers in freezer bags. Berries, grapes and drained pineapple chunks work
well too. Because of the pit, mango is a little hard to cut up, but it's easy to find
in your grocer's freezer.

Frozen fruit is good a piece at a time on its own, as a base for your favourite
smoothie, or in Fruity Milkshake, page 12, Frosty Fruit Soup, page 51, and
Bubble Juice, page 118.

Orange Mango Sparkle

*Add some sparkle to your skin and hair
with this bubbly, refreshing drink.
Good for a crowd!*

Get It Together: dry measures, blender, can opener, measuring spoons, liquid measures, 4 medium glasses, teaspoon

1.	Frozen mango slices, page 103	1 1/2 cups	375 mL
	Can of mandarin orange segments (with juice)	10 oz.	284 mL
	Honey	1 tsp.	5 mL
	Ground cinnamon, just a pinch		
2.	Lemon lime soft drink	2 cups	500 mL

1. Put the first 4 ingredients into the blender. Cover with the lid. Process for about 30 seconds until smooth. Pour 1/2 cup (125 mL) into the glasses.

2. Add 1/2 cup (125 mL) of the soft drink to each glass. Stir gently. Serves 4.

1 serving: 129 Calories; 0.3 g Total Fat (0.1 g Mono, 0.1 g Poly, 0.1 g Sat); 0 mg Cholesterol; 33 g Carbohydrate; 2 g Fibre; 1 g Protein; 16 mg Sodium

Pictured on page 105.

A Yotta Yams

*I yam what I yam—sweet and spicy at the
same time! Try these as a movie night snack with
your favourite dip, instead of potato chips.*

Get It Together: fork, oven mitts, sharp knife, cutting board, 2 large resealable freezer bags, baking sheet with sides, cooking spray, measuring spoons, dry measures, wire rack

1.	Small unpeeled yam (or sweet potato)	1	1
2.	Cooking oil	2 tsp.	10 ml
3.	Cornflake crumbs	1/3 cup	75 mL
	All-purpose flour	1 tbsp.	15 mL
	Cajun seasoning	1 tsp.	5 mL

(continued on next page)

   The Cover Story

1. Poke the fork into the yam in several places. Microwave on high (100%) for 2 minutes. Use the oven mitts to turn the yam over. Microwave for another 2 to 3 minutes until the knife tip can be inserted but the yam is still firm. Let stand for 20 minutes. Cut the yam lengthwise into quarters. Slice across the quarters to make thin, triangle-like pieces. Place the oven rack in the top position. Turn the oven broiler on. Grease the baking sheet with the cooking spray. Set aside.

2. Put the yam into 1 of the bags. Drizzle with the cooking oil. Seal the bag. Shake until coated.

3. Combine the remaining 3 ingredients in the other bag. Add 1/2 the yam. Seal the bag. Shake until coated. Arrange the yam on the baking sheet. Repeat with the remaining yam. Spray the yam lightly with the cooking spray. Broil in the oven for about 10 minutes until tender and starting to brown. Remove the baking sheet to the wire rack. Turn the oven broiler off. Serves 2.

1 serving: 368 Calories; 5.1 g Total Fat (2.7 g Mono, 1.5 g Poly, 0.4 g Sat); 0 mg Cholesterol; 76 g Carbohydrate; 8 g Fibre; 5 g Protein; 267 mg Sodium

Pictured below.

Bright Idea: For a less spicy version, use seasoned salt instead of Cajun seasoning.

Top right: Orange Mango Sparkle, page 104
Bottom: A Yotta Yams, page 104

Very Berry Dip

*You can make a frosty version of this recipe
(see below), but the "mane" way to eat this
is as a dip. Try it with slices of pancake, toast
or Cinnamon Tortilla Crisps, page 116.*

Get It Together: dry measures, measuring spoons, blender

1. Frozen mixed berries, thawed	1/2 cup	125 mL
Berry light spreadable cream cheese	1/4 cup	60 mL
Berry jam	2 tbsp.	30 mL

1. Put all 3 ingredients into the blender. Cover with the lid. Process for about
30 seconds until smooth. Makes about 1/2 cup (125 mL). Serves 1.

*1 serving: 278 Calories; 12.4 g Total Fat (3.8 g Mono, 0.5 g Poly, 6.9 g Sat); 39 mg Cholesterol;
39 g Carbohydrate; 3 g Fibre; 7 g Protein; 449 mg Sodium*

Pictured on page 107.

VERY BERRY FROZEN TREAT: Pour the dip into a paper cup. Insert
a wooden craft stick into the middle of the dip. Freeze for 3 to 4 hours until firm.

Top: Fruit & Vegetable Fun, below
Bottom: Very Berry Dip, above

Fruit & Vegetable Fun

Try this experiment the next time your friends are over to watch a movie:
put a platter of chopped fruit or vegetables beside the bowl of chips. Bet those
orange segments and banana slices disappear first!

Their bright colours make fruit and vegetables so appealing. Organize fruit
by colours to make an artist's palette, or stack up vegetable **inukshuks**[*]
on a bed of "snowy" (ranch or cucumber) dressing. Cut them in interesting
shapes—a crinkle tool is great—and don't forget the dip!

[*] The Inuit of northern Canada built giant inukshuks—stacked
stones shaped into human figures—to guide
travellers and scare caribou into ambush.

106

Go! Go! Go!
Carbohydrates for Energy

So you're in the last few minutes of the game and you've got a breakaway and you just...run...out...of...steam.

If you feel as if your batteries have suddenly died, it probably means your body has used up most of the carbohydrates from your last meal. Carbohydrates give you the sugars you need for energy, whether it's for sports or getting through that boring music practice.

Carbs come in two forms: simple and complex. Simple carbs taste sweet and are found in sugary foods, such as cookies, candies and soft drinks. They're also in fruit, vegetables and milk. Simple carbs give you quick energy, but be choosy. A piece of fruit will give you nutrients that a lollipop can't.

Complex carbs, also called starches, are found in corn, peas, rice, bread, potatoes, pasta and cereal. They take more time to break down, which means they release their energy over a longer period. Pick the whole wheat or high-fibre options in this carb category for an even better nutrient hit.

If you're healthy and active, you can choose from both types of carbs in a balanced diet. Then go burn off that energy—run, dance, touch the sky!

Banana Pancakes

Banana Pancakes

If you share this with any little monkeys at your
house you'll be the top banana!

Get It Together: dry measures, large bowl, mixing spoon, small bowl,
fork, liquid measures, measuring spoons, large frying pan, pancake lifter, cutting
board, sharp knife, serving plate, foil, 4 dinner plates

1. Pancake mix	1 1/4 cups	300 mL
2. Large egg	1	1
Banana milk	1 cup	250 mL
Peanut butter	2 tbsp.	30 mL
3. Cooking oil, approximately	1 tbsp.	15 mL
4. Medium bananas, sliced	2	2

1. Put the pancake mix into the large bowl. Dig a hole in the pancake mix with
the mixing spoon.

2. Break the egg into the small bowl. Beat with the fork until the egg is bubbly
on top. Add the milk and peanut butter. Stir well. Pour into the hole in the
pancake mix. Stir just until the pancake mix is moistened. The batter will
be lumpy.

3. Heat 1 tsp. (5 mL) of the cooking oil in the frying pan on medium-low for
3 minutes. Measure the batter into the pan, using about 1/4 cup (60 mL) for
each pancake. Cook for about 3 minutes until bubbles form on top and the
edges of the pancakes appear dry. Use the lifter to turn the pancakes over.
Cook for another 2 to 3 minutes until the bottoms are golden. Use the lifter
to check. Remove the pancakes to the serving plate. Cover with the foil to
keep warm. Repeat with the remaining batter, heating more cooking oil in
the pan before each batch if necessary so the pancakes won't stick. Makes
8 pancakes.

4. Put 1 pancake on each plate. Cover pancakes with banana slices. Top with
remaining pancakes. Serves 4.

1 serving: 339 Calories; 11.9 g Total Fat (5.5 g Mono, 3.1 g Poly, 2.4 g Sat); 66 mg Cholesterol;
49 g Carbohydrate; 3 g Fibre; 11 g Protein; 609 mg Sodium

Pictured on page 108.

Bright Idea: Instead of banana milk, make these pancakes using strawberry,
white or chocolate milk.

Funny Side Up Breakfast

Play a yolk—err, joke—on your family with this pretend-egg breakfast. Good for an after-school snack too!

Get It Together: dinner plate, measuring spoons, table knife, can opener, paper towel

1. Whole wheat bread slice	1	1
Pineapple spreadable cream cheese	3 tbsp.	50 mL
2. Canned peach half	1	1

1. Toast the bread. Place it on the plate. Spread the cream cheese in an oval shape on the toast to look like the white of a fried egg.

2. Blot the peach half dry with the paper towel. Place the peach half, cut-side down, on top of the cream cheese to look like the yolk of a sunny side up egg. Serves 1.

1 serving: 243 Calories; 16.7 g Total Fat (4.8 g Mono, 0.9 g Poly, 10 g Sat); 49 mg Cholesterol; 19 g Carbohydrate; 3 g Fibre; 6 g Protein; 282 mg Sodium

Pictured on page 111.

Strawberry French Toast

Will French toast give you the energy to study for your French class? Mais oui!

Get It Together: 9 x 9 inch (22 x 22 cm) pan, cooking spray, measuring spoons, small saucepan or small microwave-safe bowl, large bowl, liquid measures, whisk, oven mitts

1. Butter	1 tbsp.	15 mL
2. Large eggs	2	2
Strawberry milk	1/2 cup	125 mL
3. Texas bread slices	4	4

(continued on next page)

Go! Go! Go!

1. Place the oven rack in the centre position. Turn the oven on to 450°F (230°C). Grease the pan with the cooking spray. Set aside. Melt the butter in the saucepan on medium.

2. Break the eggs into the large bowl. Add the milk and butter. Beat with the whisk until the mixture is bubbly on top.

3. Dip both sides of each bread slice into the egg mixture. Arrange the bread slices in the pan to cover the bottom. Bake for about 15 minutes until golden. Remove the pan. Turn the oven off. Serves 2.

1 serving: 420 Calories; 15.1 g Total Fat (5.4 g Mono, 1.7 g Poly, 6.4 g Sat); 235 mg Cholesterol; 53 g Carbohydrate; 2 g Fibre; 17 g Protein; 693 mg Sodium

Pictured below.

Bright Idea: Instead of strawberry milk, try your favourite flavoured milk. For a special treat at Christmastime, use eggnog.

Top: Strawberry French Toast, page 110
Bottom: Funny Side Up Breakfast, page 110

Confetti Rice Wedges

Energize rice with colourful veggies, then shape it into cool triangles. Ask Mom to make extra rice one night so you can use the leftovers.

Get It Together: 2 loaf pans, plastic wrap, dry measures, large bowl, mixing spoon, small microwave-safe bowl, grater, vegetable peeler, heavy cans, sharp knife, cutting board

1. Cold cooked long grain white rice	2 cups	500 mL
Herb and garlic spreadable cream cheese	1/4 cup	60 mL
2. Frozen kernel corn	1/3 cup	75 mL
3. Grated unpeeled English cucumber	1/4 cup	60 mL
Grated peeled carrot	1/4 cup	60 mL
Chopped red pepper	1/4 cup	60 mL

1. Line 1 of the pans with the plastic wrap. Set aside. Put the rice and cream cheese into the large bowl. Stir until well mixed.

2. Put the corn into the small bowl. Microwave, covered, on high (100%) for about 1 minute until the corn is cooked. Add it to the rice mixture.

3. Add the remaining 3 ingredients. Stir well. Put the rice mixture into the pan lined with plastic wrap. Cover with another sheet of plastic wrap directly on the surface. Flatten the rice mixture with your hands. Set the bottom of the other pan on top. Put the cans in the pan for weight. Chill in the refrigerator for 2 hours. Remove the top sheet of plastic wrap. Place the cutting board on the pan with the rice mixture. Holding the pan and cutting board together, flip them carefully so the rice mixture will come out on top of the board without breaking. Remove the plastic wrap. Cut into 2 squares. Cut each square in half diagonally for a total of 4 triangles. Serves 2.

1 serving: 546 Calories; 22.7 g Total Fat (6.4 g Mono, 1.1 g Poly, 13.9 g Sat); 69 mg Cholesterol; 74 g Carbohydrate; 2 g Fibre; 12 g Protein; 306 mg Sodium

Pictured on page 112.

Why did the boy eat his homework?
Because his teacher said it was a piece of cake.

Top: Wrapped Chicken Caesar, page 114
Bottom: Confetti Rice Wedges, above

Wrapped Chicken Caesar

Wanna keep your chicken Caesar salad "under wraps?" Nestle it inside a tomato tortilla for a great-looking lunch.

Get It Together: sharp knife, cutting board, medium bowl, dry measures, measuring spoons, mixing spoons, dinner plate

1. Chopped or torn romaine lettuce, lightly packed	1 cup	250 mL
Chopped cooked chicken	1/2 cup	125 mL
Creamy Caesar dressing	2 tsp.	10 mL
2. Tomato-flavoured flour tortilla (9 inch, 22 cm, diameter)	1	1

1. Put the lettuce into the bowl. Add the chicken and dressing. Toss well.

2. Place the tortilla on the plate. Spoon the chicken mixture in a horizontal line along the middle of the tortilla. Fold the sides over the filling. Roll up from the bottom to enclose the filling inside. Serves 1.

1 serving: 397 Calories; 14.9 g Total Fat (3.7 g Mono, 3 g Poly, 3 g Sat); 66 mg Cholesterol; 37 g Carbohydrate; 3 g Fibre; 27 g Protein; 471 mg Sodium

Pictured on page 112.

Bright Idea: Wrap it the way you like it! Instead of chicken, use beef or salmon. Instead of a tomato tortilla, use a spinach or whole wheat tortilla.

Go! Go! Pizza

Share the energy of this high-carb pizza with a friend—and race through the afternoon together!

Get It Together: baking sheet, measuring spoons, sharp knife, cutting board, grater, dry measures, oven mitts

1. Prebaked pizza crust (7 1/2 inch, 19 cm, diameter)	1	1
Pizza sauce	2 tbsp.	30 mL

(continued on next page)

Go! Go! Go!

Go! Go! Pizza, page 114

2.		
Chopped cooked ham	1/2 cup	125 mL
Chopped tomato	1/4 cup	60 mL
Chopped green pepper	1/4 cup	60 mL
Grated part-skim mozzarella cheese	1/2 cup	125 mL

1. Place the oven rack in the centre position. Turn the oven on to 400°F (205°C). Place the pizza crust on the baking sheet. Use the back of the spoon to spread the pizza sauce on the crust.

2. Scatter the next 3 ingredients over the sauce. Sprinkle with the cheese. Bake for about 15 minutes until the cheese is melted and bubbling. Remove the baking sheet. Turn the oven off. Serves 2.

1 serving: 379 Calories; 10.5 g Total Fat (2.7 g Mono, 0.6 g Poly, 3.8 g Sat); 36 mg Cholesterol; 48 g Carbohydrate; 3 g Fibre; 22 g Protein; 1053 mg Sodium

Pictured on front cover and above.

Bright Idea: Instead of ham, use chicken for a great new flavour. Add extra colour and nutritional punch to your pizza with red, yellow or orange pepper.

Go! Go! Go!

Cinnamon Tortilla Crisps

A crunchy sweet snack with hints of cinnamon. These crisp a little as they cool. Serve with Very Berry Dip, page 105.

Get It Together: baking sheet. cooking spray. measuring spoons. small bowl. mixing spoon. pastry brush. cutting board. sharp knife. oven mitts.

1. Brown sugar, packed	1 tbsp.	15 mL
Ground cinnamon	1/2 tsp.	2 mL
2. Cooking oil	2 tsp.	10 mL
Whole wheat flour tortilla	1	1
(9 inch, 22 cm, diameter)		

1. Place the oven rack in the centre position. Turn the oven on to 350°F (175°C). Grease the baking sheet with the cooking spray. Put the brown sugar and cinnamon into the bowl. Stir until well mixed.

2. Brush the cooking oil on the tortilla. Sprinkle with the brown sugar mixture. Cut the tortilla into 16 wedges. Arrange on the baking sheet. Bake for about 10 minutes until the edges are golden. Remove the baking sheet. Turn the oven off. Serves 2.

1 serving: 172 Calories; 6.9 g Total Fat (3.6 g Mono, 2.3 g Poly, 0.7 g Sat); 0 mg Cholesterol; 25 g Carbohydrate; 1 g Fibre; 3 g Protein; 156 mg Sodium

Pictured on page 117.

Tortilla Sushi

When you just can't get your hands on dried seaweed sheets (the traditional sushi wrap), a spinach tortilla will get you rolling. Ask Mom to make extra rice the night before so you can use the leftovers.

Get It Together: microwave-safe dinner plate. dry measures. small bowl. measuring spoons. mixing spoon. table knife. plastic wrap. cutting board. sharp knife

1. Fresh asparagus spears	2	2
2. Cold cooked rice	1 cup	250 mL
Herb and garlic spreadable cream cheese	2 tbsp.	30 mL
Imitation crabmeat (not canned), flaked	1/2 cup	125 mL
Creamy Caesar dressing	1 tbsp.	15 mL

(continued on next page)

  Go! Go! Go!

3. Spinach flour tortilla (9 inch, 22 cm, diameter)	1	1

1. Snap the white, woody ends off the asparagus spears. Wash the spears and place them, wet, on the plate. Microwave, covered, on high (100%) for 20 to 30 seconds until softened.

2. Put the rice and cream cheese into the bowl. Mix well. Add the crabmeat and dressing. Stir.

3. Spread the crabmeat mixture on the tortilla almost to the edge. Place the asparagus on the mixture at the bottom of the tortilla. Roll the tortilla tightly around the asparagus. Wrap with the plastic wrap. Chill for about 1 hour until firm. Cut into 6 slices. Serves 2.

1 serving: 376 Calories; 11.6 g Total Fat (2.6 g Mono, 1.5 g Poly, 4.4 g Sat); 26 mg Cholesterol; 54 g Carbohydrate; 2 g Fibre; 13 g Protein; 649 mg Sodium

Pictured below.

Top: Cinnamon Tortilla Crisps, page 116
Bottom: Tortilla Sushi, page 116

Choco-Banana Spread

Spread a little of this rich, fudgy treat on a whole wheat bagel or piece of toast for a quick power boost. Or use in Ice Cream Sandwiches, page 119.

Get It Together: sharp knife, cutting board, medium microwave-safe bowl, fork, mixing spoon

1. Medium banana, sliced	1	1
2. Peanut butter	2 tbsp.	30 mL
Chocolate chips	1 tbsp.	15 mL

1. Put the banana slices into the bowl. Use the fork to mash the banana until smooth.

2. Put the peanut butter and chocolate chips on top of the mashed banana. Microwave, covered, on high (100%) for 45 to 60 seconds until the chocolate chips are softened. Stir until smooth. Store in an airtight container for up to 1 week. Makes about 2/3 cup (150 mL).

2/3 cup (150 mL): 354 Calories; 20.5 g Total Fat (9.1 g Mono, 4.8 g Poly, 5.6 g Sat); 2 mg Cholesterol; 39 g Carbohydrate; 4 g Fibre; 10 g Protein; 163 mg Sodium

Pictured on page 120.

FROSTY CHOCO-BANANA TREATS: Put the spread into 2 small paper cups. Insert a wooden craft stick into the middle of each cup. Freeze for at least 6 hours or overnight until firm.

Bubble Juice

Put a little fizz in your feet! Refreshing grape ice cubes float in bubbly juice— perfect on a sunny day.

Get It Together: liquid measures, dry measures, large glass

1. White grape juice	3/4 cup	175 mL
Club soda	1/4 cup	60 mL
Frozen small seedless grapes, page 103	1/4 cup	60 mL

(continued on next page)

Go! Go! Go!

1. Pour the grape juice and club soda into the glass. Add the grapes. Serves 1.

1 serving: 138 Calories; 0.3 g Total Fat (0 g Mono, 0.1 g Poly, 0.1 g Sat); 0 mg Cholesterol; 34 g Carbohydrate; trace Fibre; 1 g Protein; 20 mg Sodium

Pictured on page 120.

Bright Idea: Instead of club soda, use sparkling water.

What do you call a kid **w**ho can **sing** and **drink** root beer at the **same time?**

A **pop singer.**

Ice Cream Sandwiches

This scrumptious snack will have your friends and family up and running when you call them.

Get It Together: tablespoon, dry measures, small bowl, table knife, 8 x 8 inch (20 x 20 cm) pan, spatula, foil

1. Vanilla ice cream	2 cups	500 mL
2. Choco-Banana Spread, page 118		
3. Whole graham crackers	18	18

1. Put the ice cream into the bowl. Set aside to soften. Don't let it melt!

2. Make the Choco-Banana Spread according to the recipe on page 118.

3. Cover the graham crackers with the spread. Arrange 9 crackers, spread-side up, in the pan to cover the bottom. Use the spatula to spread the ice cream on the crackers in the pan. Arrange the remaining crackers, spread-side down, on top of the ice cream. Press gently. Cover with the foil. Freeze for at least 3 hours or overnight. Cut between the crackers to make 9 ice cream sandwiches.

1 sandwich: 161 Calories; 7.1 g Total Fat (2.7 g Mono, 0.9 g Poly, 3.1 g Sat); 14 mg Cholesterol; 22 g Carbohydrate; 1 g Fibre; 3 g Protein; 128 mg Sodium

Pictured on page 120.

Bright Idea: Instead of ice cream, use vanilla frozen yogurt.

Why did the **doughnut** go to the **dentist?**
It needed a **chocolate filling.**

Clockwise from
Ice Cream S
Bubble Juic
Choco-Bana

Measurement Tables

Throughout this book measurements are given in Conventional and Metric measure. To compensate for differences between the two measurements due to rounding, a full metric measure is not always used. The cup used is the standard 8 fluid ounce. Temperature is given in degrees Fahrenheit and Celsius. Baking pan measurements are in inches and centimetres as well as quarts and litres. An exact metric conversion is given below as well as the working equivalent (Metric Standard Measure).

Oven Temperatures

Fahrenheit (°F)	Celsius (°C)
175°	80°
200°	95°
225°	110°
250°	120°
275°	140°
300°	150°
325°	160°
350°	175°
375°	190°
400°	205°
425°	220°
450°	230°
475°	240°
500°	260°

Pans

Conventional Inches	Metric Centimetres
8x8 inch	20x20 cm
9x9 inch	22x22 cm
9x13 inch	22x33 cm
10x15 inch	25x38 cm
11x17 inch	28x43 cm
8x2 inch round	20x5 cm
9x2 inch round	22x5 cm
10x4 1/2 inch tube	25x11 cm
8x4x3 inch loaf	20x10x7.5 cm
9x5x3 inch loaf	22x12.5x7.5 cm

Spoons

Conventional Measure	Metric Exact Conversion Millilitre (mL)	Metric Standard Measure Millilitre (mL)
1/8 teaspoon (tsp.)	0.6 mL	0.5 mL
1/4 teaspoon (tsp.)	1.2 mL	1 mL
1/2 teaspoon (tsp.)	2.4 mL	2 mL
1 teaspoon (tsp.)	4.7 mL	5 mL
2 teaspoons (tsp.)	9.4 mL	10 mL
1 tablespoon (tbsp.)	14.2 mL	15 mL

Cups

Conventional Measure	Metric Exact Conversion Millilitre (mL)	Metric Standard Measure Millilitre (mL)
1/4 cup (4 tbsp.)	56.8 mL	60 mL
1/3 cup (5 1/3 tbsp.)	75.6 mL	75 mL
1/2 cup (8 tbsp.)	113.7 mL	125 mL
2/3 cup (10 2/3 tbsp.)	151.2 mL	150 mL
3/4 cup (12 tbsp.)	170.5 mL	175 mL
1 cup (16 tbsp.)	227.3 mL	250 mL
4 1/2 cups	1022.9 mL	1000 mL (1 L)

Dry Measurements

Conventional Measure Ounces (oz.)	Metric Exact Conversion Grams (g)	Metric Standard Measure Grams (g)
1 oz.	28.3 g	28 g
2 oz.	56.7 g	57 g
3 oz.	85.0 g	85 g
4 oz.	113.4 g	125 g
5 oz.	141.7 g	140 g
6 oz.	170.1 g	170 g
7 oz.	198.4 g	200 g
8 oz.	226.8 g	250 g
16 oz.	453.6 g	500 g
32 oz.	907.2 g	1000 g (1 kg)

Casseroles

CANADA & BRITAIN		UNITED STATES	
Standard Size Casserole	Exact Metric Measure	Standard Size Casserole	Exact Metric Measure
1 qt. (5 cups)	1.13 L	1 qt. (4 cups)	900 mL
1 1/2 qts. (7 1/2 cups)	1.69 L	1 1/2 qts. (6 cups)	1.35 L
2 qts. (10 cups)	2.25 L	2 qts. (8 cups)	1.8 L
2 1/2 qts. (12 1/2 cups)	2.81 L	2 1/2 qts. (10 cups)	2.25 L
3 qts. (15 cups)	3.38 L	3 qts. (12 cups)	2.7 L
4 qts. (20 cups)	4.5 L	4 qts. (16 cups)	3.6 L
5 qts. (25 cups)	5.63 L	5 qts. (20 cups)	4.5 L

Recipe Index

A

B

C

Recipe Index   **123**

Recipe Index

N

O

P

Q

R

S

T

U

V

W

Y

Company's Coming cookbooks are available at retail locations throughout Canada!

EXCLUSIVE mail order offer on next page

Buy any 2 cookbooks—choose a 3rd FREE of equal or lesser value than the lowest price paid.

Original Series — CA$15.99 Canada — US$12.99 USA & International

CODE		CODE		CODE	
SQ	150 Delicious Squares	MAM	Make-Ahead Meals	EB	The Egg Book
CA	Casseroles	PB	The Potato Book	SDPP	School Days Party Pack
MU	Muffins & More	CCLFC	Low-Fat Cooking	HS	Herbs & Spices
SA	Salads	CFK	Cook For Kids	BEV	The Beverage Book
AP	Appetizers	SCH	Stews, Chilies & Chowders	SCD	Slow Cooker Dinners
SS	Soups & Sandwiches	FD	Fondues	WM	30-Minute Weekday Meals
CO	Cookies	CCBE	The Beef Book	SDL	School Days Lunches
PA	Pasta	RC	The Rookie Cook	PD	Potluck Dishes
BA	Barbecues	RHR	Rush-Hour Recipes	GBR	Ground Beef Recipes
PR	Preserves	SW	Sweet Cravings	FRIR	4-Ingredient Recipes
CH	Chicken, Etc.	YRG	Year-Round Grilling	KHC	Kids' Healthy Cooking
KC	Kids Cooking	GG	Garden Greens	MM	Mostly Muffins
CT	Cooking For Two	CHC	Chinese Cooking		**NEW** September 1/06
SC	Slow Cooker Recipes	PK	The Pork Book		
SF	Stir-Fry	RL	Recipes For Leftovers		

Lifestyle Series

CODE	CA$19.99 Canada US$15.99 USA & International
DC	Diabetic Cooking
DDI	Diabetic Dinners
LCR	Low-Carb Recipes
HR	Easy Healthy Recipes

Special Occasion Series

CODE	CA$20.99 Canada US$19.99 USA & International
GFK	Gifts from the Kitchen

CODE	CA$24.99 Canada US$19.99 USA & International
BSS	Baking—Simple to Sensational
CGFK	Christmas Gifts from the Kitchen
TR	Timeless Recipes for All Occasions

Cookbook Author Biography

CODE	CA$15.99 Canada US$12.99 USA & International
JP	Jean Paré: An Appetite for Life

Most Loved Recipe Collection

CODE	CA$23.99 Canada US$19.99 USA & International
MLA	Most Loved Appetizers
MLT	Most Loved Treats
MLBQ	Most Loved Barbecuing
MLCO	Most Loved Cookies

CODE	CA$24.99 Canada US$19.99 USA & International
MLSD	Most Loved Salads & Dressings

3-in-1 Cookbook Collection

CODE	CA$29.99 Canada US$24.99 USA & International
QEE	Quick & Easy Entertaining
MNT	Meals in No Time
	NEW August 1/06

Order ONLINE for fast delivery!

Log onto **www.companyscoming.com**, browse through our library of cookbooks, gift sets and newest releases and place your order using our fast and secure online order form.

Buy 2, Get 1 FREE!

Buy any 2 cookbooks—choose a **3rd FREE** of equal or lesser value than the lowest price paid.

Title	Code	Quantity	Price	Total
			$	$
DON'T FORGET to indicate your FREE BOOK(S). (see exclusive mail order offer above) please print				

TOTAL BOOKS (including FREE)

TOTAL BOOKS PURCHASED: $

	International	Canada & USA
Shipping & Handling First Book (per destination)	$ 11.98 (one book)	$ 5.98 (one book)
Additional Books (include FREE books)	$ ($4.99 each)	$ ($1.99 each)
Sub-Total	$	$
Canadian residents add G.S.T.(7%)		$
TOTAL AMOUNT ENCLOSED	$	$

Terms
- All orders must be prepaid. Sorry, no C.O.D.'s
- Prices are listed in Canadian Funds for Canadian orders, or US funds for US & International orders.
- Prices are subject to change without prior notice.
- Canadian residents must pay 7% G.S.T. (no provincial tax required)
- No tax is required for orders outside Canada.
- Satisfaction is guaranteed or return within 30 days for a full refund.
- Make cheque or money order payable to: **Company's Coming Publishing Limited.**
- Orders are shipped surface mail. For courier rates, visit our website: **www.companyscoming.com** or contact us: Tel: 780-450-6223 Fax: 780-450-1857.

Gift Giving
- Let us help you with your gift giving!
- We will send cookbooks directly to the recipients of your choice if you give us their names and addresses.
- Please specify the titles you wish to send to each person.
- If you would like to include your personal note or card, we will be pleased to enclose it with your gift order.
- Company's Coming Cookbooks make excellent gifts: birthdays, bridal showers, Mother's Day, Father's Day, graduation or any occasion ...collect them all!

☐ MasterCard ☐ VISA Expiry ___/___ MO/YR

Credit Card # _____

Name of cardholder _____

Cardholder signature _____

Shipping Address Send the cookbooks listed above to:
☐ **Please check if this is a Gift Order**

Name: _____

Street: _____

City: _____ Prov./State: _____

Postal Code/Zip: _____ Country: _____

Tel: ( ) _____

E-mail address: _____

Your privacy is important to us. We will not share your e-mail address or personal information with any outside party.

☐ **YES! Please add me to your newsletter e-mail list.**